The author would like to thank all the clubs, associations, private fisheries, the National Rivers Authority, the National Trust, British Waterways, North West Water and the many people too numerous to mention by name, who assisted in the research of this book. Special thanks, however, for the contribution of Ken Watson of the National Rivers Authority.

In memory of a dear friend,
Frederick H. Sudworth,
23rd November 1993.

First published by:
The Bluecoat Press
Bluecoat Chambers
School Lane
Liverpool
L1 3BX

Designed by:
March design, Liverpool
Illustrations by:
John Thirsk

ISBN 1 872568 19 X

NRA

National Rivers Authority

Angling Guide to North West England

Compiled by L.W. Millington

THE BLUECOAT PRESS

Foreword

Fishing is one of the most popular pastimes, enjoyed by many thousands of people throughout the country. I feel privileged, therefore, to be the Chairman of the National Rivers Authority's North West Regional Fisheries Advisory Committee. I joined the Committee in 1992 and became the Chairman in 1993. The Committee currently consists of seventeen members representing the various groups and organisations who have an interest in fisheries. A list of the members, and who they represent, is contained within this book. Although the Committee exists only in an advisory capacity it is an important mechanism by which the views of anglers and others, who are the NRA's customers, may be fed into the decision making process.

This is a time of great change for the NRA, not only in terms of internal organisational change but also because of recent and ongoing debates on major policy issues such as funding arrangements, the national rod licence and proposals for a national coarse fish close season. In addition, the Government's intention to set up an environment agency, probably in 1996, is likely to result in further changes as the NRA's activities are transferred to the new organisation.

The funding of the NRA's fisheries service is one of the most important issues which needs to be addressed. Historically, considerable financial support has been provided by central Government through grant aid. This has reduced considerably over recent years as a consequence of tighter controls on public expenditure. The NRA, therefore, is placed in the position of funding an increasing percentage of the costs incurred by its fisheries service directly through licence duties and any other sources of income that may be identified. There is clearly a limit to the amount that you, the angler, are prepared to pay and, likewise, a limit on the standard of service that you are prepared to accept. A balance between the two must be achieved and striking the right balance is one of the biggest challenges facing the NRA's fisheries function.

Since becoming the Committee's Chairman I have emphasised the need for the NRA in the North West to improve its communication with anglers and, indeed, anyone with an interest in fisheries. It seems only fair to me that those who pay for the fisheries service should be kept fully informed of not only how their money is actually spent but also the major issues under consideration.

I hope that you will find the book to be both informative and interesting. In planning the guide we have tried to provide a good mixture of useful information on where to fish and articles of general fisheries interest.

JAMES R. CARR
Chairman, North West Regional Fisheries Advisory Committee

Contents

How Rod Licence money is spent

The charts below highlight the income and expenditure of the Fisheries Department.
Work by the Fisheries Department is funded by five main sources of income.

Grant in aid from central Government
Rod Fishing Licences
Net Fishing Licences
Income from sales and service*
Re-charge of costs to other NRA functions. (Work undertaken by fisheries staff to investigate the effects of low flows or a pollution discharge are examples of work which may be re-charged.)*

* These are shown as miscellaneous on the income/ expenditure charts.

What your licence helps to pay for

The attached Activity Analysis chart indicates what percentage of budget is spent to maintain, improve and develop salmon fisheries, trout fisheries, freshwater fisheries, and eel fisheries.

Enforcement

This includes anti-poaching work, licence checking and ensuring that byelaws are observed. It also includes the prosecution of offenders, although ultimately, a proportion of these costs are recovered. During 1993, 715 anglers were prosecuted for fishing without a licence. In addition, offenders were prosecuted for 138 byelaw and other offences. Fisheries legislation exists to protect fish stocks and therefore is of benefit to anglers.

Fish rearing and stocking

The NRA operates purpose built fish hatcheries. Fish reared are used to restock rivers following pollution incidents and to compensate for developments such as reservoirs which can reduce river flows and hamper the migration of fish. Restocking is used to up grade rivers, together with improvements to water quality and fish habitats. During 1993/94, 1,780,000 fish were stocked in the North West.

Monitoring

Regular monitoring and surveys of salmonid and coarse fish stocks involve the use of electric fishing, netting, fish counters and traps, and the use of catch statistics. The information is used to help to assess the health of fish stocks and to identify and solve problems caused by pollution, low flows, barriers to migration or disease. It also gives us the necessary information to follow trends in fish populations and to comment on the proposals of third parties.

Income

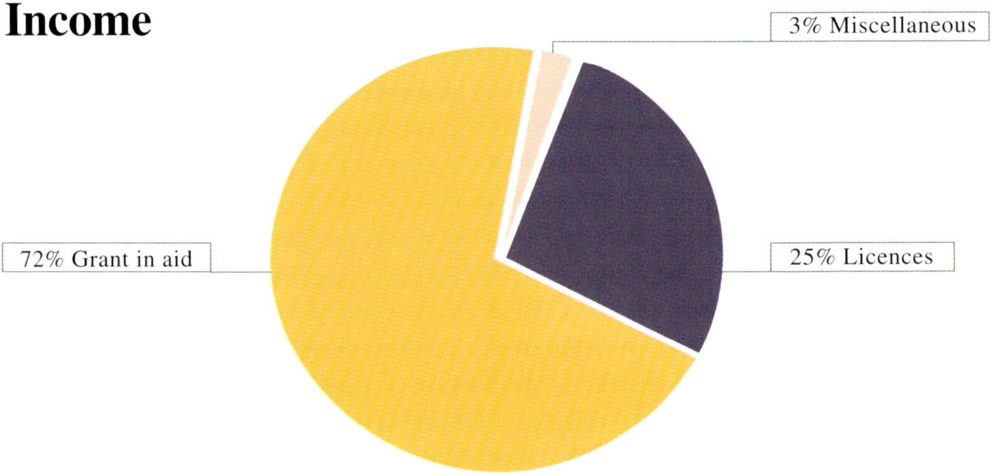

Fisheries regulation

The NRA is required to regulate fishing, including angling and netting, by a system of licences. The legislative framework is continually evolving. Orders, byelaws and licence duties have to be reviewed and Government approval obtained.

Fish mortalities

Fisheries staff often mount rescue operations to save fish threatened by pollution, drought and other causes. It may be necessary to remove the fish and place them elsewhere. Occasionally, special equipment is used to bubble air into the water during the pollution event to help fish survive. If fish are killed, fisheries staff assess the numbers and species lost and remove them if possible. Whenever possible, we recharge the cost of investigation and restocking to the polluter.

Promotion and advice

Consultation and liaison with angling and riparian interests is done at all levels nationally, through regional or local advisory committees, angling clubs or with individual owners or anglers as necessary. Advice is given to fishery owners, managers and angling clubs on many aspects of fishery management or fishing.

Physical and chemical improvements

Often, the cause of poor fish stocks is impoverished habitat. Improvements can often be made by providing cover or reintroducing features such as pools and riffles in rivers. Suitable spawning areas can be created or, for salmon and sea trout in particular, access to spawning areas can be improved by removal of obstructions or by constructing fish passes. If pollution or water abstraction is found to be the cause of poor fish stocks, NRA fisheries staff will work together with other NRA departments to find a solution.

Planning and development

The Fisheries Department is involved in drawing up river catchment management plans. It is also responsible for screening all proposals potentially affecting rivers to ensure that fisheries are not adversely affected. Such proposals include planning and development proposals, proposals to undertake river engineering works, proposals to abstract or discharge water and proposals to introduce fish.

Research and development

Research is presently being carried out in a number of areas to increase the overall effectiveness and efficiency of the function. In particular methods are being developed to measure the size of fish stocks, determine factors affecting fisheries' performance and how best to rehabilitate streams and rivers.

Expenditure

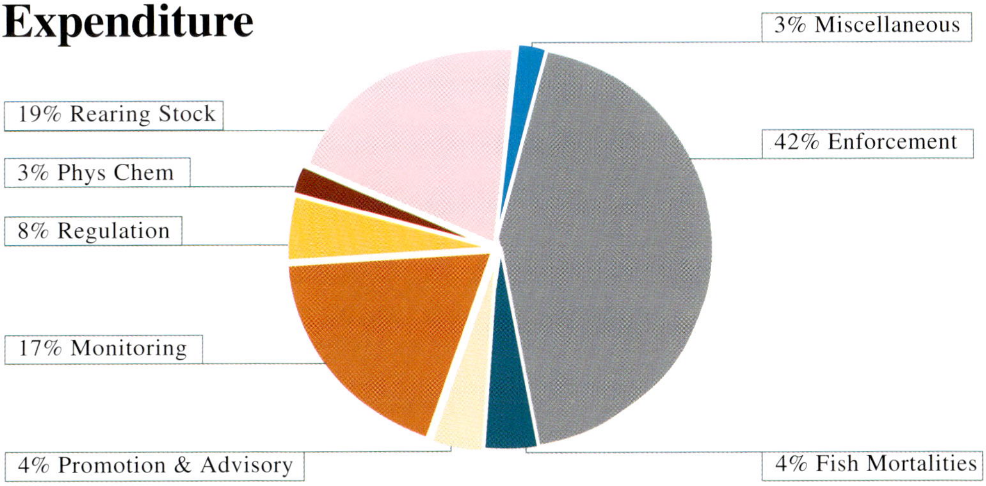

A Day in the Life of a Bailiff

Wednesday 1st June

0530 hrs

The day began like many others, with the call of an over-enthusiastic alarm. With sleepy eyes and weary limbs, its noise was silenced. NRA Water Bailiff A72 was awake - well, sort of!

0630 hrs

Washed, fed, dressed and in my car, heading for the river. It was June 1st and the close season for coarse fishing on rivers in this part of the world, but that doesn't always stop anglers finding a secluded spot and enjoying a bit of illegal sport. The local "hot spots" produced no anglers at all, but the river was in fine fettle and I picked out three barbel lying flank to flank, either preparing to, or having just spawned. The larger fish, probably the female, was a fair fish indeed, so I noted the pool in my notebook, in case we should need to collect broodstock for the hatchery later in the year.

0830 hrs

Arrived at the area depot to meet the rest of the bailiff team. The team comprises a Fisheries Inspector, Senior Bailiff, and three Bailiffs. There was a job organised for that day, and after a short briefing from the Fisheries Inspector, we loaded the Landrover and trailer with all the necessary equipment, and headed off to a water in our area. We were netting a lake of approximately three acres to remove as many freshwater fish as possible, returning only trout. This involved laying two 100 metre nets side by side across the middle of the pool, pulling them away from each other, and hopefully entrapping the fish at each end. This type of operation involves the use of a boat, ropes, drysuits and a fair amount of effort before any fish are successfully caught.

1330 hrs

Lunch break. Our Inspector was settling down to take the first bite of a well earned sandwich when his pager sounded. It proved to be the first of four reports of fish in distress and, unknown to us, this call was to dictate the pattern of work for the next five days! As a Bailiff Team, we have to respond to any calls of fish in distress, which are usually reported by members of the public. The first response is to dispatch somebody to assess the situation. On this occasion, our Inspector went. It was about an hour and a half later, while we were netting the second pool of the day, that we received a call to return to the depot, as the Landrover could be needed to carry aeration equipment. We packed up and headed back.

1600 hrs

Turned into the depot drive. Within minutes, two of us were on our way in different directions to investigate two further incidents, while the others re-loaded the Landrover with aeration equipment, in case it should be needed.

Left: Fish rescue. Right: A bailiff checking rod licences. Far right: Bailiffs with equipment seized from poachers.

The first call was a pollution resulting in half a dozen dead roach and sticklebacks. It had affected the river which would require monitoring, but no immediate action to save further fish was necessary because the discharge had been stopped. A Bailiff colleague was on his way to a reported slurry spillage. A tractor towing a tanker full of slurry had overturned, releasing its contents towards the river. This incident was potentially a serious problem for a premier river fishery and, for this reason, the aeration equipment was being loaded at the depot. Meanwhile, I was on my way to a reported drain-down. A farmer had pumped water from a small pool to irrigate his land. The report stated that the pool was very low, and that the fish were running out of water. This could have meant performing a "fish rescue", but in the event this proved unnecessary, as the farmer had stopped pumping, and the fish were in no immediate danger. I telephoned the depot, and reported my findings. I was instructed to head for home, but to be ready to come out at short notice, as the slurry incident was ongoing.

1720 hrs
Finished work.

2100 hrs
The telephone rang. The fourth incident of the day had occurred, and it was to prove by far the most serious. It was another pollution incident involving slurry. The earlier incident had been relatively minor, with a small amount of slurry of weak concentration entering, but not affecting, the river. In the latest incident an accident on a farm had caused the rupture of a slurry tank, releasing thousands of gallons of raw slurry. If not contained, tens of thousands of fish and miles of river would be wiped out. The Bailiff Team were called out and worked continuously throughout the night to save the fish stocks. Under torch and Landrover spotlight, we placed aerators in the river, hoping that they would supply enough oxygen, should problems occur.

0130 hrs Thursday
Drove fifty miles to collect more aerators, and by first light we had seven aerators running in the river. After a break of only three hours that Thursday I finally booked off at 1935 hrs.

0730 hrs Friday
Returned to the aerator site, and for the next three nights worked one sixteen hour shift and two twelve hour shifts.

It is fair to state that Wednesday 1st June was not a typical day, because it included a major pollution incident. However, in many other ways it is typical. An NRA Bailiff's work is varied, often unexpected and can involve long hours. The pollution incident, due to actions of NRA staff from several functions combined with the remedial actions of the farmer himself, was halted before any damage to the river environment occurred. No fish were lost.

News Round-up

Rivercall

The National Rivers Authority has launched a new service for people using the North West's rivers for recreation. By calling the Rivercall line on 0891 500 999 people can get up-to-date information on flow levels on rivers across the region. A recorded message, which is updated once a day, gives the latest river conditions based on the level of flow above or below normal summer levels. The message also indicates if flow levels are rising, steady or falling.

The new telephone service has been launched by the NRA in response to demand from river users ranging from anglers to canoeists. The information on river flows is taken from NRA radio monitoring stations across the region. These stations are also used by the NRA to monitor flows for its Flood Warning Service. The twelve stations providing information for the Rivercall service are:

River Eden - Kirkby Stephen, Appleby, Warwick Bridge

River Lune - Killington, Caton

River Ribble - Locks Weir, Jumbles Rock, Samlesbury

River Weaver - Ashbrook

River Dane - Rudheath

River Irwell - Bury Bridge

River Goyt - Marple Bridge

Calls to the new service are charged at 39p per minute cheap rate and 49p per minute at all other times.

Mike Knowles, Rivercall project leader said: "The NRA has been receiving an increasing number of calls from river users seeking information about flow levels so that they can plan activities like fishing, canoeing and walking. The new Rivercall service provides a quick and easy way for them to get the information they need.

"We will be closely monitoring the Rivercall service and if it proves successful, we may consider increasing the number of rivers it covers." A leaflet with a detachable card bearing the Rivercall number has been produced and copies are available from Public Relations. Mike is urging NRA staff to try out the service and to let him have their views and comments on it.

Restocking Lancashire Rivers

Fish stocks in Lancashire rivers have been given a major boost by Central Area fisheries staff. Over recent months, they have released thousands of coarse fish reared at the Leyland fish hatchery into five rivers - the Lune, Ribble, Wyre, Calder and Douglas. The huge restocking exercise, which involved 90,000 fish, is part of the authority's effort to maintain and improve fish stocks in the region's rivers. The NRA in the North West releases more fish than any other NRA region - in 1993/4, fisheries staff reared 1,377,000 fish and released 1,780,000 into rivers. Of the fish released, 1,587,000 were salmon and sea trout and 193,000 were coarse fish. The hatchery at Leyland is where the NRA rears its coarse fish and it is the local rivers which will benefit from the latest re-stocking exercise. Around 10,000 dace and 10,000 chub have been released into the River Calder to mitigate for stocks reduced by industrial pollution. The same numbers have been released into the Wyre which has a shortage of spawning grounds for these two species of fish. Around 7,500 chub and 7,500 dace have been released into the River Ribble to compensate brood stock (pregnant fish) which were taken from the river and stripped of their eggs at the Leyland hatchery. The eggs are reared to provide fish for restocking across the region. A total of 20,000 chub have been released into the River Douglas. 5,000 of these were marked with a blue dot as part of an experiment to assess the possibility of re-populating some areas of the river where water quality is improving. 15,000 dace have been released into the River Lune to boost existing stocks which appear to have declined greatly in recent years.

Jonathan Shatwell, Area Fisheries and Recreation Manager said: "This is part of our on-going programme to maintain and re-establish fish stocks in Lancashire's rivers. We keep a very close watch on the health and welfare of fish in our rivers and try to maintain stocks in areas where water quality and habitat will support them."

Biological Water Quality Survey

Biologists from the National Rivers Authority are preparing for a major project to sample the invertebrate life of rivers and canals. The result of their work at 7,000 survey sites across England and Wales during 1995 will contribute to the NRA's important five yearly assessment of environmental water quality. NRA scientists will monitor the presence of benthic macro invertebrates - small organisms such as the larvae of mayflies and caddis flies, snails, shrimps and worms which live in or on the bed of the river. Vital to the food chain, these organisms influence the aquatic life of the river as a whole. Each species thrives best under a narrow range of environmental conditions, reacting to changes that occur in its surroundings. The variety and abundance of benthic communities in a river can therefore point to the quality of the water and can often help to identify specific pollution problems which may not be detected by chemical analysis. The last major survey of water quality in England and Wales was carried out by the NRA in 1990. This was the first time that comprehensive data on the biological health of the rivers and canals of England and Wales has been recorded in a consistent way. Once 1995 data on invertebrates has been collected, the NRA will be able to build up a picture of the changing biology of rivers and canals for the first time. Viewed alongside changing patterns of chemical quality, this information will add considerably to the NRA's understanding of the factors influencing the quality of the water environment. John Seager, NRA Head of Environmental Quality explained: "There has been a progressive improvement in the chemical quality of rivers and canals in England and Wales in recent years. However, used on its own, chemical quality assessment might allow a river to achieve a good grading, but still have poor aquatic life. With the inclusion of biological assessment, the 1995 survey will allow us to develop a much better picture of the changing quality of our rivers and canals in terms of both their chemistry and biology." The NRA's approach to water quality assessment is based on its General Quality Assessment (GQA) scheme. The GQA concept is a series of separate but complementary assessments which provide different "windows" on water quality. Key components of the GQA scheme are chemical and biological assessments, but the NRA plans to introduce further "windows" looking at nutrient levels and aesthetic quality in the future. Data on these two aspects of water quality will be collected for the first time in 1995, although assessments will not be made as classification methods are still under development. Results of the 1995 biological survey will allow rivers and canals to be assigned "biological grades" in the same way that the NRA already grades rivers and canals according to their chemical quality. Biological grading will be based on scores derived from the number and range of benthic macro-invertebrates found on each stretch of river or canal. For example, epherema danica, the fisherman's mayfly, which survives only in the cleanest water would achieve a high score. Oligochaeta (freshwater worms) and chironomidae (non-biting midge larvae) which can tolerate poorer water quality would attract lower scores. The final grading would be assessed by comparing how closely the score for the observed biology matches the score that would be expected at that site under natural and unpolluted conditions. The latter score can be predicted using a computer programme called RIVPACS (River Invertebrate Prediction and Classification System) which was developed by the Institute of Freshwater Ecology and is used by the NRA. The full report of the NRA's five yearly General Quality Assessment of rivers and canals in England and Wales in 1995, including both chemical and biological assessments, will be published in 1996.

The Ribble Fisheries Management Plan

Viscount Mills, Area Fisheries Recreation and Ecology Manager in NRA North West's Central Area reports on a scheme that aims to return the river to the level of its heyday.

The Ribble catchment is the largest and most diverse river system within the Central Area of the NRA's North-West Region. The Ribble has four major tributaries - The Hodder, Calder, Darwen and Douglas - and supports major rod and line fisheries for both coarse and game fish as well as net fisheries for salmon and sea trout in the Ribble estuary. In the past, the Ribble provided significant harvests of salmon, a catch of over 15,000 fish being recorded in 1867. However, industrial pollution decimated the salmon fishery during the last quarter of the 19th century and by 1900, catches were almost non-existent. It was not until 1930 that stocks began to recover but they have never reached former levels. Rod catches of Ribble salmon and sea trout show a slightly increasing trend from 1972 to 1991. Nevertheless, while rod catches of salmon on the Ribble were at a similar level to those on the Lune and Eden until 1981, since then they have been considerably lower. Add to this the reduction in both fishing effort and catches during the three consecutive dry summers of 1989, 1990 and 1991 and it is not surprising that by the beginning of 1992, the prevailing mood of Ribble fishermen was pessimistic. Consequently, the NRA decided to produce a plan designed to identify clearly the issues affecting Ribble fisheries, their inter relationships and the strategy needed to address them. The Ribble Fisheries Management Plan was launched as a consultation document on 1 September, 1992. It provided riparian owners, anglers and netsmen with a clear and unequivocal statement as to what the NRA proposed to do as well as giving an opportunity for all these groups to put forward their own views. Considerable progress had been made in addressing many of the plan's targets. Key achievements to date are as follows:

- A comprehensive review of the historical catch data for Ribble salmon and sea trout.
- The introduction of a log-book scheme to record catches of both migratory salmonids and coarse fish.
- Extensive electric fishing surveys of the upper and middle Ribble as well as the Hodder, Calder and Douglas catchments.
- The construction of a new fish counter and trap at Waddow Weir on the Ribble.
- The completion of a new salmon and sea trout hatchery capable of supplying all the Ribble's stocking needs.

The timescale of the plan is five years and many targets still need to be met. There has been a notable improvement in water quality throughout the catchment but much remains to be done in relation to water quantity. Predation by cormorants and competition from stocked brown trout is being investigated. Up until now, the NRA's programme of fisheries improvements and developments in the Ribble system has concentrated on the stocking of migratory salmonids. In the future, however, there will be an equal emphasis placed on habitat restoration and enhancement. Overall, the plan has provided a focus for the NRA, fisheries associations, fishermen, and environmental organisations to work towards the common goal of maintaining, improving and developing Ribble fisheries. As such, it heralds the introduction of NRA catchment management plans which are now progressively being drawn up for all major river systems in England and Wales.

Tender Loving Care

If the fish reared at the NRA's Leyland Fish Farm could speak, they would call Rod Taylor "Daddy". Thousands upon thousands of coarse fish are reared at the farm and thrive on Rod's tender loving care before they are released into the region's rivers. The Leyland Fish Farm was established several years ago as concern was growing about the diminished stocks of coarse fish in some of the North West's more polluted rivers. A major review of the role of Leyland Fish Farm was recently carried out. The future production will be chub, dace and barbel for restocking rivers. Priority will be given to restoring fish populations after pollution incidents and to waters where significant improvements in water quality have taken place. Under careful management, the Leyland farm has flourished and is constantly breaking new ground through experiments designed to encourage the fish to spawn. The farm is one of just two NRA coarse fish farms and is believed to be the only one in the country using mains water to supply the fish hatchery. Because it is virtually unique, setting up the farm was no easy task for Rod and his assistant, John Stone. Most of the fish farming equipment available is designed for game fish farms which rear salmon and trout — fish for which there is a much more developed market. Rearing coarse fish is a very different operation and much of the equipment at the Leyland fish farm has either been adapted or, as with the filter system necessary to keep the water pure, designed from scratch. The system may not be high tech, but it is certainly innovative. Old fashioned nylon pan scrubs act as a filter to remove algae from the water in one tank. John said: "You need to be a chemist, a biologist and an engineer to do this job!" As Spring - breeding season for the fish - approaches, Rod and John with the help of the bailiff team collect "brood stock" from the rivers. These are the fish which will be used to parent the many thousands of offspring which will be nurtured at the farm until they themselves are old enough to be released into the wild. Some of the fish reared at the Leyland farm are kept until they are old enough to spawn themselves. Timing is all-important in the fish farming game, as Rod will testify. "Chub and dace spawn only once a year, producing between 8,000 to 10,000 eggs per fish depending on their body weight, so you only get one chance to get it right." Adult fish are caught before they are due to spawn and are taken to the fish farm where the males and females are put into separate tanks. Their reproductive cycle is then controlled by the use of light and temperature. Rod and John can induce spawning by gradually increasing the temperature of water in the holding tanks and the amount of light entering them over a period of days. This gives the fish the impression that Spring — the breeding season — is approaching. By experimenting in this way, Rod has discovered that by using light to control the cycle, female barbel can be encouraged to produce eggs at the rate of a new batch every 15 days — cutting out the "hit and miss" element of catching spawning wild coarse fish which only spawn annually. When the female fish have ovulated, they are "stripped" of the eggs. To ensure that this process causes as little distress to the fish as possible, they are anaesthetised. Once the eggs have been collected, the sperm taken from the male fish is added. The fertilised eggs are put into jars through which a constant supply of clean water passes. When the eggs hatch out, the tiny fish are transferred to tanks, where for a few days they survive on the nutrients contained in the egg sac which is still attached to their bellies. Once this has been used up, the fish swim up to the top of the tank, hungry for their first real feed. The feeding of the fish plays an important part in their development. Fish feed more in warm waters and in the hatchery, which is heated, fish are kept in almost semi-tropical conditions to encourage them to eat more and grow at a faster rate. The intensive feeding continues when the fish are transferred out of doors to the nine lagoons behind the hatchery. Here, in addition to the diet of nutrient rich pellets, the fish start to feed on the zooplankton carefully cultivated in the ponds to give them a taste for what would be part of their staple diet in the wild. After two years in the pond, the fish are ready to be transferred to their new homes in rivers across the North West. As they get their first taste of freedom, back at Leyland Rod and John are busy starting the cycle all over again ...

Consultative Associations

The National Rivers Authority, North West Region works closely with the many angling clubs in the area. There is a statutory requirement on the NRA to set up and maintain a Regional Fisheries Advisory Committee. The purpose of this Committee is for the NRA to liaise with representatives of the fishing fraternity. In the North West, prospective members of RFAC are nominated by the region's eight Fisheries Consultative Associations. National Rivers Authority Head Office appoints the Committee chairperson, following recommendation from the Regional General Manager and agreement with the Ministry of Agriculture, Fisheries and Food. The Regional General Manager appoints the remaining members of RFAC from those nominated, and they usually serve for three years. In appointing members to the Committee an attempt is made to balance the varying north/south, coarse/game and sport/commercial interests. Further information on the Consultative Associations can be obtained from the secretaries. Two of these Associations are described below.

The Ribble Fisheries Association

This Association was established in 1951 to protect the interests of all anglers, angling clubs and riparian owners in the Ribble system. It represents several thousand coarse and game anglers on virtually all parts of the catchment. Pollution, water abstraction and welfare of fish stocks

continue to be the main concerns and the Association works closely with the NRA in attempting to deal with these. In recent years conservation has become a major issue. The Association believes that the stock level of the Ribble is not in a position to support unrestricted angling for some species. Therefore, the Association asks all salmon anglers to release fish caught during the month of October. In addition, the Association would like to see a season limit put on the number of salmon that may be taken by individual anglers. The Association feels that this is the best way to ensure as much natural spawning and regeneration as possible. To advance this improvement, most members of the association contribute financially to the Ribble and Hodder Salmon Propagation Fund which pays for the stocking of salmon smolts in both rivers each year. This, along with the NRA's stocking policy is beginning to produce results.
K.B. Spencer
(Chairman)

The River Eden and District Fisheries Association

This Association, with a membership of local clubs, individual anglers and riparian owners provides for a combined approach in pursuing beneficial policies and protecting the interests of angling. The Association was formed in 1951, on the inception of the Cumberland River Board, at the invitation of the Ministry of Agriculture, Fisheries and Food for the purpose of looking after fisheries interests in this area. It is asked to nominate persons to serve on the RFAC and representatives also attend the annual liaison meetings organised by the NRA. The views of the members raised at the Association's regular meetings are taken up by the RFAC representative. All members are kept fully informed of these activities and are encouraged to participate. Pollution and anti-field sport groups present ongoing problems to the angler. Local societies and clubs do excellent work on behalf of their members, but a united approach can sometimes produce a more satisfactory outcome.
L. Henrys
(Secretary and Treasurer)

Consultative Associations Contacts

Eden & District Fisheries Association

Mr L. Henrys
3 Mill Bank
Low Heskett
Carlisle, CA4 OHJ

Esk & Liddel Fisheries Association

Mr B. Jones
Overesk
Watchhill Park
Canonbie
Dumfriesshire, DG14 OTD

Furness & South Cumbria Fisheries Association

Mr D. E. Lancaster
Wetherlam
Mount Pleasant
Ulverston, LA12 7RF

Lancashire Fisheries Association

Mr A. G. R. Brown
10 Dale Road
Golborne
Warrington

Lune & Wyre Fisheries Association

Mr R. A. Challenor
c/o Davis & Bowring
6 Main Street
Kirkby Lonsdale, nr. Carnforth

Mersey & Weaver Fisheries Association

Mr B. J. Briggs
151 Moss Lane
Swinton
Manchester

Ribble Fisheries Association

Mr K. B. Spencer
36 Heap Street
Burnley, BB10 IRL

South & West Cumbria Fisheries Association
Mr E. M. Wright
Low Orchard
Haile
Egremont
Cumbria

NRA Fisheries staff

Regional Fisheries, Conservation, Recreation and Biology Manager
Dr M. Diamond
Richard Fairclough House
Knutsford Road
Warrington, WA4 IHG
Telephone (01925) 653999

Senior Fisheries Scientist
Dr M. W. Aprahamian
Richard Fairclough House
Knutsford Road
Warrington, WA4 IHG
Telephone (01925) 653999

Northern Area

Area Fisheries, Conservation, Recreation Manager
Mr N. C. Durie
Chertsey Hill
London Road
Carlisle
Cumbria, CAI 2QX
Telephone (01228) 25151

Fisheries & Recreation Manager (North Cumbria)
Mr S. Douglas
Chertsey Hill
London Road
Carlisle
Cumbria, CA1 2QX
Telephone (01228) 25151

Fisheries & Recreation Manager (South Cumbria)
Ms E. Black
Chertsey Hill
London Road
Carlisle
Cumbria, CAI 2QX
Telephone (01228) 25151

Fisheries Inspector (Eden)
Mr K. Kendall. (01228) 25151

Fisheries Inspector (West Cumbria)
Mr D. P. McCartan. (01228) 25151

Fisheries Inspector (South West Cumbria)
Mr D. A. Pearson. (01228) 25151

Fisheries Inspector (River Kent)
Mr P. Foster. (01228) 25151

Central Area

Area Fisheries, Conservation and Recreation Manager
Viscount C. P. R. Mills,
Lutra House
Dodd Way, off Seedlee Road
Walton Summit
Bamber Bridge
Preston, PR5 8BX
Telephone (01772) 39882

Fisheries & Recreation Manager
Mr J. Shatwell
Lutra House
Dodd Way, off Seedlee Road
Walton Summit
Bamber Bridge
Preston, PR5 8BX
Telephone (01772) 39882

Fisheries Inspector (Lune)
Mr S. P. Horner. (01772) 39882

Fisheries Inspector (Ribble)
Mr M. Swindells. (01772) 39882

Southern Area

Area Fisheries, Conservation and Recreation Manager

Mr A. R. Lee,
Mirwell,
Carrington Road,
Sale, M33 5NL
Telephone (0161) 973 2237

Fisheries & Recreation Manager

Mr B. M. Chappel,
Mirwell,
Carrington Road,
Sale, M33 5NL
Telephone (0161) 973 2237

Fisheries Inspector (Cheshire And Wirral)

Mr G. E. Bridgeman. (0161) 973 2237

Fisheries Inspector (Manchester)

Mr N. Taylor. (0161) 973 2237

Regional Fisheries Advisory Commitee

The Regional Fisheries Advisory Committee meets four times a year, and is an opportunity for the National Rivers Authority to consult angling organisations. Members of the committee are appointed by the NRA from nominations by the Fisheries Consultative Associations and are chosen to represent the varying fisheries interests in the region.

Chairman

Mr J. R. Carr
Moorhouse Hall
Warwick on Eden
Carlisle, CA4 8PA

Members

Mr D. Bridgewood
Nutgill Cottage
Ingleton
via Carnforth, LA6 3DS

Mr A. G. R. Brown
10 Dale Road
Golborne
Warrington

Mr J. M. Castle
Elpha House
Carnforth
Lancashire, LA6 IAA

Mr T. R. Glover
31 Preston Road
Southport, PR9 9EE

Mr S. Griffiths
18 Manor Road
Lymm
Cheshire, WA13 OAY

Mr B. N. Irving
11 Avon Close
Morton West
Carlisle, CA2 6RT

Mr K. J. Lambert
79 Prospect Road
Whalley Road
Altham West
Accrington, BB5 SDH

Mr R. F. Langley
1 Mallowdale Avenue
Heysham
Morecambe
Lancashire, LA3 2ES

Mr E. D. Le Cren
New Garbridge
Roman Road
Appleby
Cumbria, CA16 6JB

Mr S. G. Payne
Green Dyke
Dean
Workington
Cumbria, CA4 4TH

Mr K. B. Spencer
36 Heap Street
Burnley, BB10 1RL

Mr R. Tinkler
58 Glendale Rise
Carlisle
Cumbria

Mr W. M. Wannop OBE JP
Westwinds
Parkbroom
Carlisle
Cumbria, CA6 4QH

Mr R. E. Weston
Orchard Grange
8 The Park
Christleton
Chester, CH3 7AR

Mr H. Whittam
29 Lyndhurst Road
Ulverston
Cumbria, LA12 OEG

Northern Area

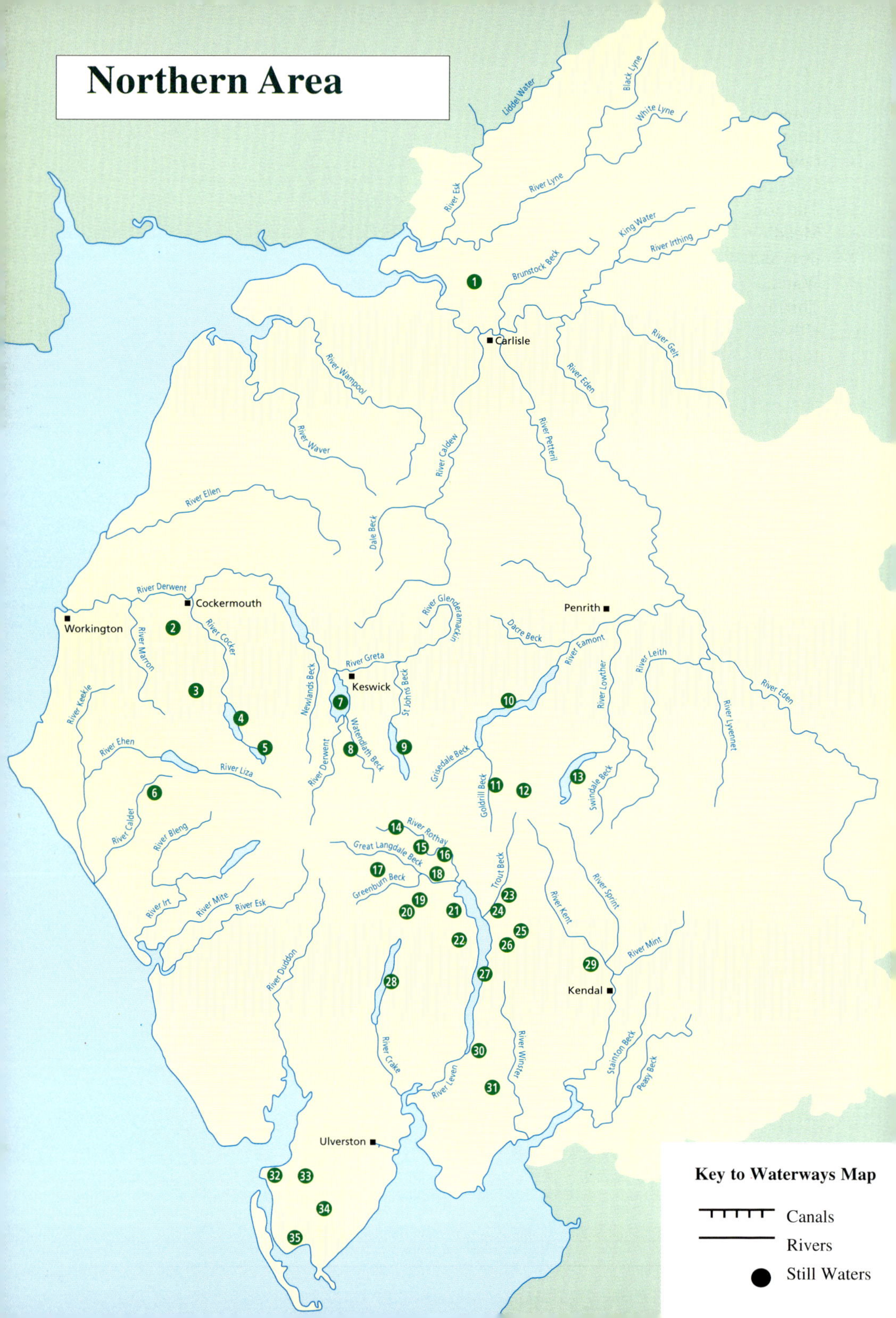

Index to Still Waters

Northern Area Still Waters

Blea Tarn

Langdale
The National Trust
Trout and Freshwater fish
Day ticket from Mrs Myers,
Blea Tarn Farm,
Langdale

Blelham Tarn

The National Trust
Trout and Freshwater fish
Day ticket from Mr F. Hilton,
(Hawkshead Angling Club)
Hawkshead Co-op,
Main Street,
Hawkshead

Brotherswater

The National Trust
Trout
Free fishery to NRA Rod Licence holders

Burlington Lake

Dalton-in-Furness
Furness Fishing Association (Game Section)
Rainbow Trout
Day ticket available from local tackle shops.
Annual permit from the Secretary of Furness Fishing Association, (Game Section)

Buttermere

National Trust
Trout, Char, Pike, Perch
Day ticket from Mr & Mrs Parker,
Dalegarth, Buttermere
also from Lothians,
Main Street, Cockermouth

Cleabarrow Tarn

Windermere, Ambleside and District Angling Association
Tench, Mirror Carp, Common Carp
No keepnets, carp sacks or ground bait allowed.
Limited access for ambulant disabled anglers.
Permit valid for Cleabarrow Tarn only, available from local tackle dealers.
Day ticket

Coniston

The National Trust
The National Trust do not own the fishing rights
Trout, Char, Pike, Perch
Enquiries should be made in the area, with reference to day tickets

Crummock Water

National Trust
Trout, Char, Pike, Perch, Sea Trout, Salmon
Day ticket from Mrs R. Beard,
Rannerdale Farm,
Buttermere,
also from Lothians,
Main Street, Cockermouth

Derwentwater

The National Trust
Pike, Perch, Brown Trout, Salmon
Day ticket from Temples,
Station Road, Keswick

Derwentwater

Keswick Anglers Association
Brown Trout, Salmon, Pike, Perch
Day ticket/Annual permit

Dubbs Reservoir Trout Fishery

Windermere, Ambleside and District Angling Association
A seven acre reservoir containing *Brown and Rainbow Trout*
Fly fishing only and a two fish limit.
Ease of access for ambulant disabled anglers.
Day ticket/Permits available from Ings Service Station (A591) or local tackle shops

Easedale Tarn

The National Trust
Freshwater fish
Free fishery to NRA Rod Licence holders

Eller Beck Fishery

Eller Beck Farm,
Brigham,
Cockermouth
3/4 acre lake containing *Roach, Tench, Carp, Bream, Trout*
Ease of access for disabled anglers, ambulant and non-ambulant. This venue is suitable for blind anglers if accompanied. Toilet facilities.
Day ticket

Ghyll Head Trout Fishery

Windermere, Ambleside and District Angling Association
11 acre reservoir containing *Brown and Rainbow Trout*
Fly fishing only; there is a two fish limit, but catch and release is encouraged using barbless hooks.
Ease of access for disabled anglers.
Day ticket for Ghyll Head only, from Beech Hill Hotel and local tackle shops

Grasmere

Windermere, Ambleside and District Angling Association
Pike, Perch, Eels (Catch and return)
Ease of access for ambulant disabled anglers.
Day ticket/7 day permit and Year permits are available from Tourist Information Centres and local tackle shops

Haweswater

Bampton, Cumbria
North West Water Ltd
Freshwater fish
No maggots or loose feeding.
Free to NRA Rod Licence holders

Hayeswater Reservoir

Penrith Angling Association
Trout
Fly fishing only
Day ticket from
C.R. Sykes, Tackle Shop,
Great Dockray, Penrith

High Arnside Tarn

Windermere, Ambleside and District Angling Association
Brown and Rainbow Trout
Fly fishing only, two fish limit. Catch and release is encouraged using barbless hooks.
Day ticket/7 day and Year permit are available from Tourist Information Centres and local tackle shops

High Newton Reservoir

Windermere, Ambleside and District Angling Association
10 acre reservoir containing *Brown and Rainbow Trout*
Fly fishing only, with a two fish limit. Catch and release is encouraged using barbless hooks.
Day ticket valid for High Newton only, available from Beech Head Hotel and local tackle shops

Holehird Tarn

Windermere, Ambleside and District Angling Association

Mixed fishery

Four acre reservoir, all fish to be returned.

Day ticket valid for Holehird Tarn only, available from Plantation Bridge Filling Station (A591) and local tackle shops.

Check with permit agent before fishing that the fishery is open.

Longton Pond Fishery

Mr C. Bowman, Crosshill Cottage, Blackford, Carlisle, CA6 4DU

Bream, Carp, Chub, Tench, Perch, Dace, Roach

Day tickets are available and must be purchased before fishing from:
Mr & Mrs Yeomans,
5 Smallstown Terrace,
Longton (next to water),
or P. Wilson Fishing Tackle,
36 Portland Place,
Carlisle
Annual permit obtainable from:
Mr C. Bowman,
Crosshill Cottage
Blackford, Carlisle

Loughrigg Tarn

The National Trust

Pike, Perch

Day Ticket from
Mrs Murphy, Tarn Foot Farm

Loweswater

The National Trust

Brown Trout, Freshwater fish,

There is no spinning or bait fishing until June 16th, and no fishing at all from 31st October until 15th March

Day ticket from Mr & Mrs Leck,
Water End Farm, Loweswater
also Lothians,
Main Street, Cockermouth

Meadley Reservoir

Cleator Moor, Cumbria
Mr W. Morley, Mr R. Moyle
142 Blowthorne Road
Cleator Moor, Cumbria

Rainbow and Brown Trout

Fly fishing only

Ease of access for disabled anglers, ambulant and non-ambulant

Day ticket/Annual permit

Middle North

Dalton-in-Furness
Furness Fishing Association (Game Section)

Rainbow Trout

Fly Fishing only

Annual permit from the Secretary of Furness Fishing Association (Game Section)

Moss Eccles Tarn

Windermere, Ambleside and District Angling Association

Brown Trout

Fly fishing only, two fish limit. Catch and release is encouraged using barbless hooks.

Day ticket from the Tower Bank Arms, Near Sawrey, also from local tackle shops

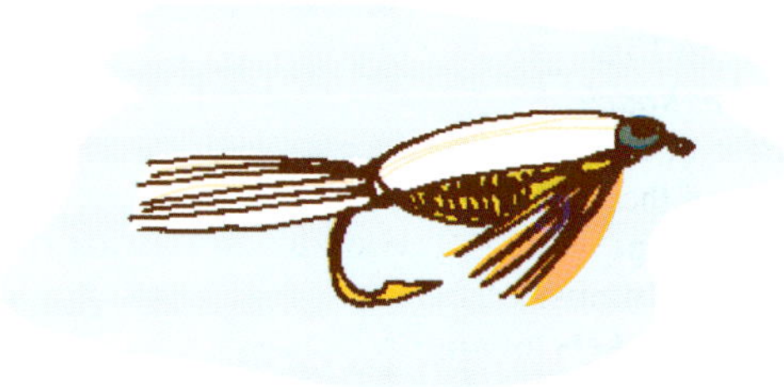

Nigel Pond

Dalton-in-Furness
Furness Fishing Association (Game Section)

Rainbow Trout

Day ticket available from local tackle shops.
Annual permit from the Secretary of Furness Fishing Association (Game Section)

Ormsgill Reservoir

Barrow-in-Furness
Furness Fishing Association (Coarse)
This is a twenty-five acre lake containing
Carp, Roach, Perch, Pike, Bream
Ease of access for ambulant disabled anglers.
Annual permit only to residents of South Cumbria. There are a limited number of day tickets on application only, none sold on the bankside

Ratherheath Tarn

Windermere, Ambleside and District Angling Association
Five acre tarn
Mixed fishery
Day ticket for Ratherheath Tarn only, available from Plantation Bridge Filling Station (A591) and local tackle shops.
Before fishing check with permit agent that fishery is open. All fish to be returned.
Open for match booking contact:
The Hon Treasurer, Mr C. Sodo
Telephone (0153) 9432463

Roanhead Complex

3 miles from Barrow-in-Furness
Furness Fishing Association (Coarse section)
This complex is made up of five waters from $^1/_2$ an acre to 13 acres containing
Carp, Roach, Perch, Pike, Tench, Bream
Ease of access for ambulant disabled anglers on two of the ponds.
Annual permits only available to residents of South Cumbria. There are a limited number of day tickets on application only. None sold on the bankside

Rydal Water

Windermere, Ambleside and District Angling Association
Pike, Perch, Eels, all fish to be returned
Day ticket/Seven day permit and Year permits are available from Tourist Information Centres and local tackle shops

School Knott Tarn

Windermere, Ambleside and District Angling Association
Rainbow Trout
Fly fishing only, two fish limit
Day ticket/7 day permit and Year permits are available from Tourist Information Centres and local tackle shops

Thirlmere

North West Water Ltd
Mr P. Guy, Recreation and Conservation Officer
Telephone (01772) 822200
Natural fishery
No maggots or loose feeding
Parking and toilet facilities
Free to NRA Rod Licence holders

Ullswater

The National Trust
Pike, Perch, Brown Trout
Free to NRA Rod Licence holders

Watendlath

The National Trust
Trout
Day tickets from Mrs Richardson, Fold Head Farm, Watendlath
Charges on request

Windermere

The National Trust
Trout, Char, Perch, Pike
Free to NRA Rod Licence holders

Yew Tree Tarn

The National Trust
Trout only
Permits from
Coniston & Torver Angling Club,
Shop 3, Lakeland House,
Tilberthwaite Avenue,
Coniston

Northern Area Rivers

River Brathay

Windermere, Ambleside and District Angling Association
Trout
Day Ticket/7 Day permit and Year permit from the Tourist Information Centres and local tackle shops

River Caldew

Carlisle Angling Association
Dace, Chub, Salmon, Trout, Sea Trout, Grayling
Day ticket/Week permit/Annual permit

Dacre Beck

Penrith Angling Association
Trout
Fly fishing only
Day ticket/Annual permit from
C.R. Sykes, Tackle Shop
Great Dockray, Penrith

River Derwent

Keswick Anglers Association
Trout, Salmon
There is limited access for ambulant disabled anglers.
Day ticket/Annual permit

River Eamont

Penrith Angling Association
Trout
Fly fishing only
There is limited access for ambulant disabled anglers.
Day ticket/Annual permit from
C.R. Sykes, Tackle Shop
Great Dockray, Penrith

River Eden

Penrith Angling Association
Trout
Fly fishing only
Day ticket/Annual permit from
C.R. Sykes, Tackle Shop,
Great Dockray, Penrith

River Eden

Carlisle Angling Association
Dace, Chub, Salmon, Trout, Sea Trout, Grayling
Day ticket/Week permit/Annual permit

River Gelt

Brampton Angling Association
Trout
Day ticket/Annual permit

River Gowan

Staveley
Staveley and District Angling Association
Brown Trout, Sea Trout, Salmon
Day ticket/Week permit/Annual permit

River Greta

Keswick Angling Association
Trout
There is limited access for ambulant disabled anglers.
Day ticket/Annual permit

River Irthing

Brampton Angling Association
Trout
Day ticket/Annual permit

River Kent

Staveley
Staveley and District Angling Association
Brown Trout, Sea Trout, Salmon
Day ticket/Week permit/Annual permit

River Lowther

Penrith Angling Association
Trout
Fly fishing only
Day ticket/Annual permit from
C.R. Sykes, Tackle Shop
Great Dockray, Penrith

River Petterill

Penrith Angling Association
Trout
Fly fishing only
Day ticket/Annual permit from
C.R. Sykes, Tackle Shop
Great Dockray, Penrith

River Rothay

Windermere, Ambleside and District Angling Association
Trout
Day ticket/7 Day permit and Year permit available from Tourist Information Centres and local tackle shops

Trout Beck

Penrith Angling Association
Trout
Fly fishing only
Day ticket/Annual permit from
C.R. Sykes, Tackle Shop
Great Dockray, Penrith

Central Area

Index to Still Waters

1 Villa Lakes
2 Holemere Tarn
3 Red Well Fishery
4 New Tarn Houses
5 Stocks Reservoir
6 Briarcroft Fishery
7 Jenkinsons Lake
8 Woodford Farm Fishery
9 Barns Fold Waters
10 Higher Lickhurst Coarse Fishery
11 Haslam Park
12 Longton Brickcroft
13 Leisure Lakes
14 Cuerden Valley Park Lake
15 Runshaw Hall Lodge
16 Cricket Field Lodge
17 Shale Holes
18 Croft Lodge
19 Abbey Village Top Lodge
20 Anglezarke Reservoir
21 Rivington Reservoir
22 Adlington Reservoir
23 Abbey Lake
24 Dickens Street Lodge
25 Dean Clough Reservoir
26 Parsonage Reservoir
27 Super Street Lodge
28 Clarendon Street Lodge
29 Drakeshead Fishery
30 Cockers Lodge
31 Butts Mill Lodge
32 Fern Gore Lodges
33 Mitchell House Reservoir
34 Haggs Reservoir
35 Kearns Allen Lodge
36 Sunnyhirst Hey Reservoir
37 Entwistle Reservoir
38 Sabden Reservoir
39 Gawthorpe Hall Pond
40 Lower Foulridge Reservoir
41 Ballgrove Lake
42 Bulls Grove Lake
43 Coldwell Reservoir
44 Walverden Reservoir
45 Cant Clough Reservoir
46 Cliviger Fish Ponds

Central Area Still Waters

Abbey Lake

Nr Orrell, Wigan
Lymm Angling Club
3 acre lake containing *Tench, Bream, Roach, Pike*
Day Ticket/Annual Permit
Matches may be booked by other Clubs

Adlington Reservoir

Worthington, Nr. Wigan
Wigan and District Angling Association
Carp, Tench, Roach, Bream, Trout
Limited access for ambulant disabled anglers.
Day ticket/Annual permit

Anglezarke Reservoir

Rivington, Nr Horwich
North West Water
Mr P. Luff, Access and Recreation Manager
Freshwater fish, Trout
Limited access for disabled due to high banking.
Day ticket

Arley Reservoir

Worthington, Wigan, Greater Manchester
Wigan and District Anglers Association
Carp, Roach, Bream, Tench, Trout
Limited access for ambulant disabled anglers.
Day ticket/Annual permit

Audley Reservoir

Accrington and District Fishing Club
Rainbow Trout, Brown Trout
Annual permit

Ballgrove Lake

Winewall, Nr Colne
Pendle Borough Council
Bream, Carp, Roach, Tench, Perch, Gudgeon
Ease of access for disabled anglers, ambulant and non-ambulant.
Day ticket available from Bailiff on the bank

Barns Fold Waters

Mr F. Casson, Barns Fold Lane,
Goosnargh, Nr Preston
Telephone (01995) 651583
Rainbow Trout
Fly Fishing only
Ease of access for disabled anglers, ambulant and non-ambulant.
Day ticket/Annual Permit

Briarcroft Fisheries

(Two waters) St Michael's on Wyre
Mr P. Ashcroft,
Briarcroft Road, St Michael's
Telephone (01995) 8258
Both waters contain *Carp, Tench, Bream, Roach, Rudd*
Ease of access for disabled anglers, ambulant and non-ambulant. This venue is suitable for blind anglers if accompanied.
Day ticket

Bulls Grove Lodge

Nelson
Mr S. Heap,
Pendle Borough Council
Recreation Department
Telephone (01282) 871470
Carp, Bream, Tench, Roach
Ease of access for disabled anglers, ambulant and non-ambulant. There are fishing platforms to facilitate wheelchairs.
Day ticket/Annual permit

Butts Mill Lodge Pond

Great Harwood
Hyndburn and Blackburn Angling Association
Roach, Bream, Carp, Perch
Ease of access for disabled anglers, ambulant and non-ambulant. This venue is suitable for blind anglers if accompanied.
Annual permit

Cant Clough Reservoir

Hurstwood, Burnley
Mitre Angling Club
Trout
Annual permit/Day ticket

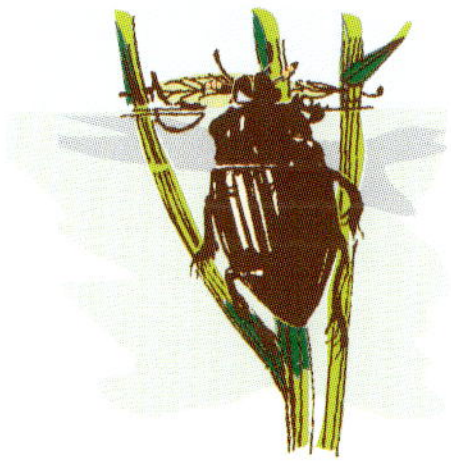

Clarendon Street Lodge

Hyndburn and Blackburn Angling Association
Roach, Tench, Bream, Perch, Carp, Pike
Annual permit

Cliviger Fishponds

Burnley
Todmorden Angling Society
Two ponds, both contain *Roach, Rudd, Bream, Tench, Crucian Carp, Brown Trout*
The bottom pond is also stocked with *Barbel, Golden Orfe, Common, Mirror & Leather Carp, Koi & Ghost Carp*
Ease of access for ambulant disabled anglers.
Open all year round
Day ticket/Annual Permit

Cockers Lodge

Oswaldtwistle
Hyndburn and Blackburn Angling Association
Roach, Tench, Bream, Perch, Carp, Pike

Coldwell Reservoir

Southfield
Coldwell Inn Activities Centre
Trout
Three fish limit
Ease of access for disabled anglers, ambulant and non-ambulant. Handicapped visitors will have the opportunity to use one of the free tickets held by the centre, and Nelson Angling Club.
Day ticket

Cricket Field Lodge

Lower Wheelton
Withnell Angling Club
Carp, Roach, Perch, Tench, Crucian Carp
Annual permit

Croft Lodge

Brinscall
Withnell Angling Club
Carp, Roach, Bream, Tench, etc.
Annual permit

Cuerdon Valley Park Lake

Lancashire Wild Life Trust
Carp, Tench, Bream, Roach, Pike, Perch
Ease of access for disabled anglers, ambulant and non-ambulant.
Day Ticket

Dean Clough Reservoir

Great Harwood
Lancashire Fly Fishing Association
Trout
Annual permit/Day ticket available from Hydburn Angling and Darts Centre, Accrington

Dickens Street Lodge

Blackburn
Hyndburn and Blackurn Angling Association
Roach, Tench, Bream, Perch, Carp, Pike
Annual permit

Drakeshead Fly Fishery

Brinscall, Nr Blackburn
Mrs Halstead, Telephone (01254) 831363
Brown and Rainbow Trout
Ease of access for disabled anglers, ambulant and non-ambulant.
Day ticket

Drakeshead Coarse Fishery

Brinscall, Nr Blackburn
Mrs Halstead, Telephone (01254) 831363
Carp Fishery
Ease of access for disabled anglers, ambulant and non-ambulant.
Day ticket

Entwistle Reservoir

North West Water Ltd
Mr P. Luff,
Recreation and Conservation Manager
Telephone (01204) 696118
Freshwater fish
Ease of access for ambulant disabled anglers.
Toilet facilities
Day ticket

Fern Gore Lodges

Accrington
Hyndburn and Blackburn Angling Association
Roach, Tench, Bream, Perch, Carp, Pike
Annual permit

Gawthorpe Hall Pond

Padiham, Lancs
Marsden Star Angling Society
Carp, Bream, Tench, Roach, Perch
Ease of access for ambulant disabled anglers.
Annual Permit

Haggs Reservoir

Accrington and District Fishing Club
Tench, Rudd, Roach, Perch, Bream
Ease of access for disabled anglers, ambulant and non-ambulant.
Annual permit

Haslam Park

Preston Borough Council
Freshwater fish
Ease of access for disabled anglers, ambulant and non-ambulant.
Free to NRA Rod Licence holders

Higher Lickhurst Coarse Fishery

Mrs Bailey,
Higher Lickhurst Farm,
Goosnargh, Nr Preston, PR3 2ER
Three acre lake containing *Carp, Tench, Bream, Roach, Perch, Pike*
Ease of access for disabled anglers, ambulant and non-ambulant. Toilet facilities.
Pre-booking welcomed.

Holmere Tarn

Carnforth
Carnforth and District Anglers Association
Rainbow Trout
(Winter fly fishing only)
Annual permit/Day or Weekly permits are available from
Mr I.K. McCartney,
20 Coniston Road, Carnforth,
Lancashire, LA5 9AZ

Jenkinsons Lake

Mr Collinson,
Jenkinsons Farm,
Wyreside Fishery, St Michaels
Carp, Bream, Roach, Rudd, Tench
Ease of access for disabled anglers, ambulant and non-ambulant. Toilet facilities.
Day ticket

Kearns Allen Lodge

Baxenden
Hyndburn and Blackburn Angling Association
Roach, Tench, Bream, Perch, Carp, Pike
Annual permit

Knotts Lane Ponds

Colne, Lancs
Marsden Star Angling Society
Carp, Bream, Tench, Roach
Ease of access for ambulant disabled anglers.
Annual permit

Leisure Lakes

Mere Brow, Nr Southport
Telephone (01772) 612226
Freshwater fish
Ease of access for disabled anglers, ambulant and non-ambulant. Wheelchair pegs. Toilet facilities.
Day ticket/Annual permit

Longton Brickcroft

(South Pond), Drumacre Lane, Longton, Preston
Longton & District Angling Society
Mirror, Common & Wild Carp, Tench, Roach, Rudd, Bream, Perch, Pike, Chub, Eels
Ease of access for disabled anglers, ambulant and non-ambulant.
Day ticket/Annual Permit

Lower Foulridge Reservoir

Nr Colne
Mr S. Heap
Pendle Borough Council Recreation Department
Telephone (01282) 871470
Carp, Roach, Tench, Bream
Ease of access for ambulant disabled anglers
There is no close season, but no keep-nets are allowed from 15th March to 15th June inclusive, except for matches.
Day ticket

Mitchell's House Reservoir

Accrington and District Fishing Club
Brown Trout, Rainbow Trout
Fly fishing only
Day ticket/Annual permit

New Houses Tarn

Horton in Ribbleside
Manchester Anglers Association
Trout
Fly fishing only
Annual permit

Parsonage Reservoir

Blackburn
Bowland Game Fishing Association
Rainbow Trout, Freshwater fish
Annual permit/Day ticket available from Row Lee Tackle Box, Blackburn

Red Well Fishery

Over Kellett
Carnforth
Four acre lake containing *Carp, Tench, Bream, Roach, Rudd, Perch*
Ease of access for disabled anglers, ambulant and non-ambulant.
Toilet facilities
Day ticket

Red Well Fishery

Over Kellett
Carnforth
Small pool containing *Rainbow Trout*
Any method
Ease of access for disabled anglers, ambulant and non-ambulant.
Toilet facilities
Day ticket

Rivington Reservoir (Lower)

Chorley
First Organization,
First Rivington, Anderton
Freshwater fish, Trout
Limited access for disabled anglers due to high banking.
Day ticket

Rivington Reservoir (Upper)

Chorley
First Organization,
First Rivington, Anderton
Freshwater fish
Ease of access for disabled anglers, ambulant and non-ambulant
Day ticket

Roddlesworth Reservoir (Upper)

Horwich Fly Fishing Club
Trout
Fly fishing only
Access for disabled anglers by prior arrangement to First Organization,
First Rivington,
Anderton
Day ticket/Annual permit

Roddlesworth Reservoir (Lower)

Abbey Village
Withnell Angling Club
Trout, Freshwater fish
Day ticket/Annual permit

Runshaw Hall Lodge

Euxton
Withnell Angling Club
Tench, Roach, Rudd, Carp, Bream
Annual permit

Sabden Reservoir

Accrington and District Fishing Club
Rainbow Trout, Brown Trout
Annual permit

Shale Holes

Brinscall
Withnell Angling Club
Carp, Bream, Tench, Roach, etc.
Ease of access disabled anglers, ambulant and non-ambulant.
Day ticket/Annual permit

Slate Pits Reservoirs 1, 2 and 3

Accrington
Hyndburn and Blackburn Angling Association
Roach, Tench, Bream, Perch, Carp, Pike
Annual permit

Stocks Reservoir

Ribble Valley
Mrs R. Currie,
The Trout Farm, Low Mill,
Bentham, Lancaster
Brown and Rainbow Trout
Fly fishing only
Ease of access for ambulant disabled anglers.
Day ticket/Annual permit

Sunnyhurst Hey Reservoir

Darwen
North West Water
Mr P. Luff,
Recreation and Conservation Manager
Mixed fishery
Day ticket

Super Street Lodge

Clayton-le-Moors
Hyndburn and District Angling Association
Roach, Tench, Bream, Perch, Carp, Pike
Annual permit

Top Lodge

Chorley
Withnell Angling Club
Tench, Bream, Roach, Carp, Chub, Rudd
Annual Permit

Top Lodge at Abbey Mill

Withnell Angling Club
Tench, Bream, Carp, Roach, Rudd, Perch
Annual permit

Villa Trout Lake

The Villa, Borwick Lane,
Dockacre, Carnforth
Trout
Fly fishing only
Ease of access for disabled anglers, ambulant and non-ambulant.
Toilet facilities
Day ticket/Annual permit

Villa Coarse Lake

The Villa, Borwick Lane,
Dockacre, Carnforth
Freshwater fish
Ease of access for disabled anglers, ambulant and non-ambulant.
Toilet facilities
Day ticket/Annual permit

Walverden Reservoir

Pendle, Lancashire
Mr P. Heap,
Pendle Borough Council, Recreation Department
Carp, Bream, Roach, Tench
Ease of access for ambulant disabled anglers.
Day ticket/Annual permit

Woodfold Farm Fisheries

Mr John Cornthwaite,
Woodfold Farm, Whitechapel,
Goosnargh, Preston
Telephone (01995) 40347
There are five seperate fishing pools, three contain *Roach, Perch, Tench, Carp*. The other two pools contain *Bream, Roach, Chub*
Ease of access for ambulant disabled anglers. The intention is to make access for wheelchairs in the future.
Day ticket

Worthington Reservoir

Wigan, Greater Manchester
Wigan & District Angling Association
Carp, Roach, Bream, Tench, Trout
Limited access for ambulant disabled anglers.
Day ticket/Annual permit

Central Area Rivers

River Calder

Accrington and District Fishing Club
This club has two stretches on the River Calder which are Martholme and Dunkirk Hall Farm, Read.
Chub, Dace, Roach, Pike, Trout
Annual permit

River Calder

Hyndburn and District Angling Association
This association has 8 stretches on the Calder which are as follows:
Workhouse Farm, Simonstone
Altham Bridge
Coppins Farm, Whalley
Orchard, Whalley
Factory, Whalley
Calderstone, Whalley
Little Mitton Farm, Whalley
Hacking Hall Farm, Billington
All these stretches of the river contain *Chub, Dace, Roach, Pike, Trout.*
Annual permit

Clapham and Austwick Beck

Ingleborough Estate, Clapham
There is limited access for ambulant disabled anglers.
Weekly permit/Annual permit

River Doe

Ingleton Angling Association
Brown Trout, Sea Trout, Salmon
Day ticket/Weekly permit/Annual permit

River Doe

Mitre Angling Club
Brown Trout, Grayling, Sea Trout, Salmon, Freshwater fish
Annual permit

River Greta

Burton-in-Lonsdale
Accrington and District Fishing Club
This club has three stretches of the river.
Annual permit

River Hodder

Bashall Eaves
Bowland Game Fishing Association
Brown, Rainbow Trout, Sea Trout, Salmon, Freshwater fish
Annual permit

River Hodder

Chaigley,
Dunsop Bridge,
Newton
Lancashire Fly Fishing Association
Trout, Sea Trout, Salmon, Grayling
Annual permit

River Hodder

Chaigley,
Edisford Hall Estate
Salmon, Sea & Brown Trout, Grayling, Chub
Contact:
Townson Bros.,
Pendle Trading Estate,
Chatburn,
Clitheroe

River Hodder

Higher Hodder Bridge to Hodder Foot
Nr Whalley
Padiham and District Angling Society
Game and Coarse fish
Annual permit

River Keer

Carnforth
Carnforth and District Anglers Association
Brown Trout, Sea Trout
Annual permit/Day and Weekly tickets available from
Mr I.K. McCartney
20 Coniston Road
Carnforth
Lancashire, LA5 9AZ

River Lune

Crook of Lune,
Caton
The Countryside Officer,
Lancaster City Council
Trout and Salmon
Ease of access for disabled anglers, ambulant and non-ambulant. There are purpose built ramps for wheelchairs and facilities to assist the disabled including toilets.
Day ticket

River Lune

Halton and Skerton
NRA North West
Chub, Roach, Pike, Dace, Trout, Salmon
Day ticket from Mr Shallis,
Halton Stores,
St Wilfreds Park,
Halton,
Lancashire, LA2 6PN
Also from Mrs Curwen,
Greenup Cottage,
Hornby Road,
Caton, Lancs.

River Lune

Lowgill
Bowland Game Fishing Association
Brown, Rainbow Trout, Sea Trout, Salmon, Freshwater fish
Annual permit

River Lune

Kirkby Lonsdale, Tebay
Lancashire Fly Fishing Association
Trout, Sea Trout, Salmon, Grayling
Annual permit

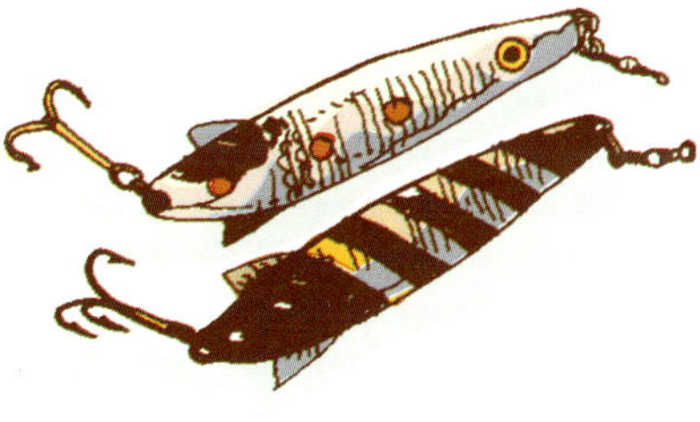

River Lune

Kirkby Lonsdale
Kirkby Lonsdale Angling Association
Salmon, Sea & Brown Trout
Annual permit/Weekly permits for hotel guests

River Ribble

Accrington and District Fishing Club
This club has two stretches of the River:
Henthorn and Sunderland Hall, Balderstones
Both contain *Chub, Dace, Pike, Perch, Trout, Sea Trout, Salmon*
Annual permit

River Ribble

Low Moor Grindleton, Wheatley Farm
Bowland Game Fishing Association
Brown, Rainbow Trout, Sea Trout, Salmon, Freshwater fish
Annual permit

River Ribble

Paythorne, Long Preston
Bowland Game Fishing Association
Brown, Rainbow Trout, Sea Trout, Salmon, Freshwater fish
Annual permit

River Ribble

Left Bank, Long Preston
Long Preston
Padiham and District Angling Society
Game and Coarse fish
Annual Permit

River Ribble

Edisford Hall Estate
Edisford Bridge to Mitton Bridge
Salmon, Sea & Brown Trout, Grayling, Chub
Contact: Townson Bros.,
Pendle Trading Estate,
Chatburn,
Clitheroe

River Ribble

Hodder Foot to Starling Brook
Nr Whalley
Padiham and District Angling Society
Salmon, Sea Trout, Trout, Grayling, Coarse fish
Day ticket/Annual permit

River Ribble

Mitton Bridge to Calderfoot
NRA North West
Roach, Chub, Pike, Dace, Trout, Salmon, Migratory Trout
Day ticket from
Mrs M. Haynes,
Mitton Hall Farm,
Mitton, Nr Whalley,
Lancs

River Ribble

Mitre Angling Club
Brown Trout, Sea Trout, Salmon, Grayling, Freshwater fish
Annual permit

River Ribble

10.5 miles down stream bank,
Horton-in-Ribblesdale
Manchester Anglers Association
Trout
Fly fishing only
Annual permit

River Ribble

Hyndburn and Blackburn Angling Association
The Association has two stretches of the Ribble:
Hacking Hall Farm, Billington
Edisford Bridge, Clitheroe
Chub, Dace, Trout, Salmon, Sea Trout
Annual permit

River Ribble

Hurst Green, 1.5 miles
Warrington Anglers Association
Chub, Roach, Dace, Trout, Sea Trout, Salmon, Gudgeon
Annual permit

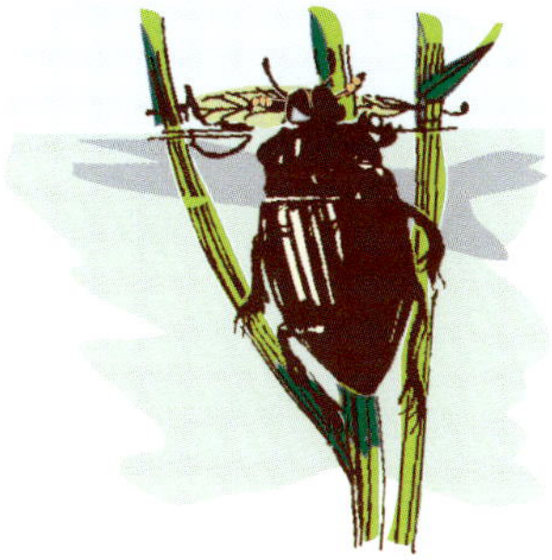

River Ribble

Ribchester, Gisburn
Lancashire Fly Fishing Association
Trout, Sea Trout, Salmon, Grayling
Annual permit

River Twiss

Ingleton Angling Association
Brown Trout, Sea Trout, Salmon
Day ticket/Week permit/Annual permit

River Wenning

Haze Hall Farm,
Clapham Station
Accrington and District Fishing Club
Brown Trout, Sea Trout, Salmon
Annual permit

River Wenning

Clapham
Bowland Game Fishing Association
Brown, Rainbow Trout, Sea Trout, Salmon, Freshwater fish
Annual permit

River Wenning

Bentham Angling Association
Brown Trout, Sea Trout, Salmon
Day ticket

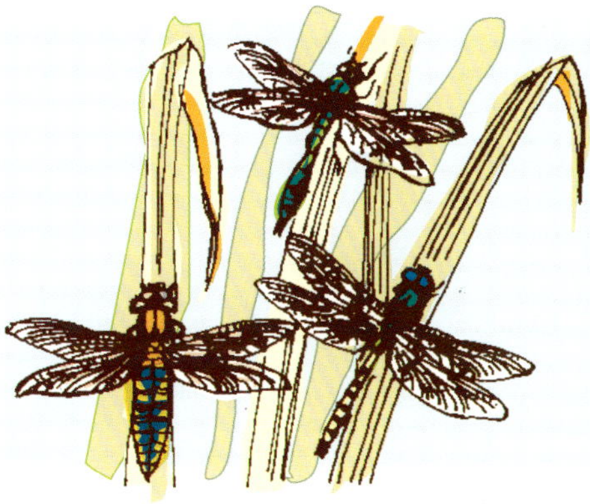

River Wyre

Churchtown, 1.5 miles
Warrington Anglers Association
Chub, Roach, Perch, Bream, Trout, Sea Trout, Salmon
Limited access for ambulant disabled anglers.
Annual permit

Southern Area

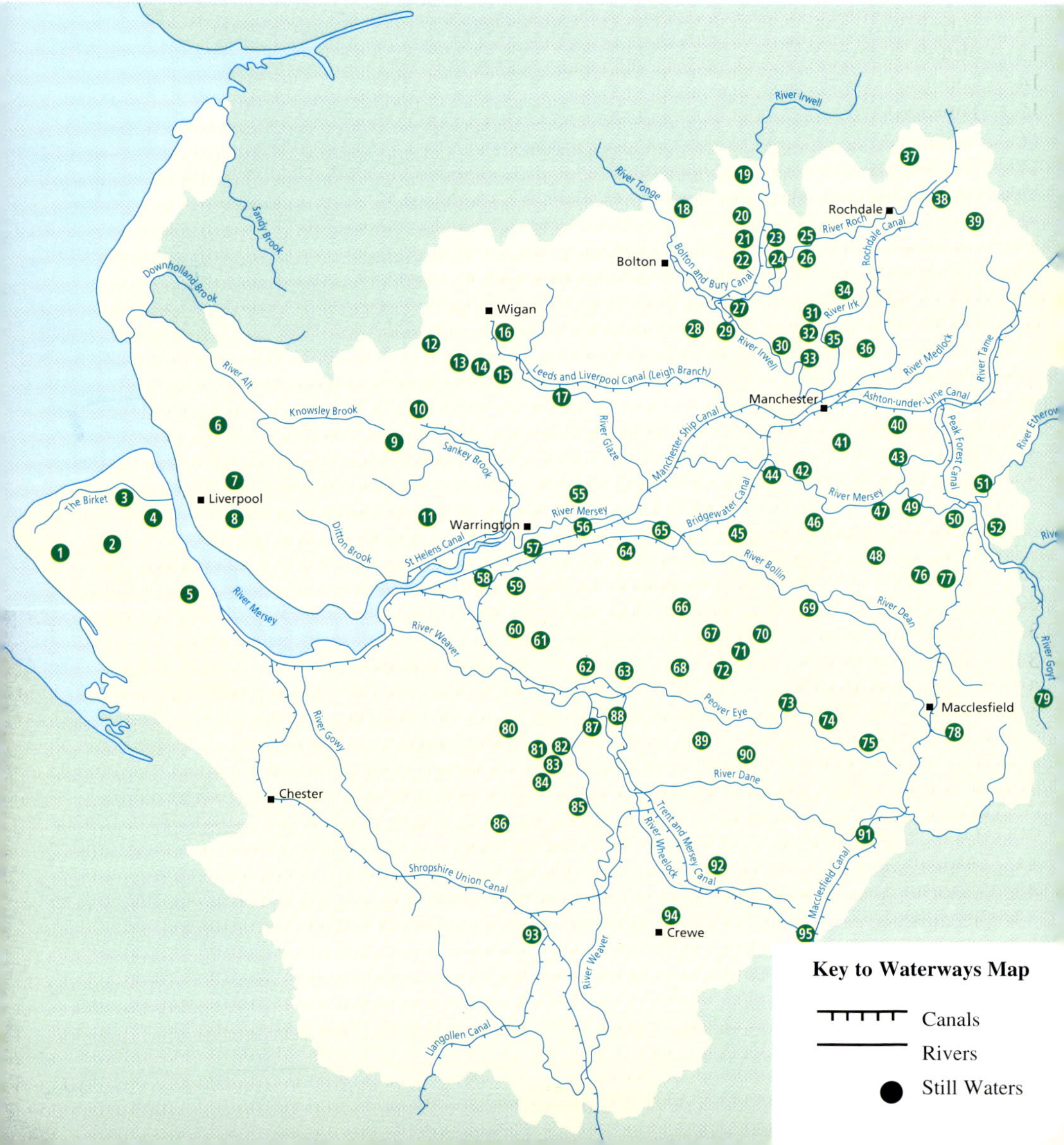

Index to Still Waters

1 Royden Park
2 Arrowe Park
3 Captains Park
4 Birkenhead Park Lower Lake
5 The Recreation Pond
6 Walton Hall Park Lake
7 Newsham Park Lake
8 Sefton Park Lake
9 Leg O'Mutton Dam
10 Carr Mill Dam
11 Bold Pool
12 Orrell Park Lake
13 Middle Place Lodges
14 Landgate Lodges
15 Three Sisters Lake
16 Widdows Flash
17 Fir Tree Flash
18 Jumbles Reservoir
19 Endcrofts Pond
20 Hazel Hall Lane
21 Coffin Lodge
22 Parkers Elton Vale
23 Claredon New Water
24 Gigg Lane Paper Works
25 Taylor And Nicholsons
26 Cromptons
27 Kirklees Carcus
28 Sand Hole Reservoir
29 Clifton Marina
30 Drinkwater Park Lake
31 Dam Head Lodge Reservoir
32 Know Mill Water
33 Clowes Park
34 Humphries Lake
35 Top And Bottom Waters
36 Boggart Hole Clough Lake
37 Watergrove Reservoir
38 Hollingworth Lake
39 Piethorne Reservoir
40 Gorton Reservoir
41 Alexandra Park Lake
42 Chorlton Water Lake
43 Reddish Vale Pond
44 Sale Water Park
45 King George V Pool
46 Abney Park Lake
47 Platt Fields Park Boating Lake
48 New House Farm Pool
49 Woodbank Park Pool
50 Compstall Lodge
51 Etherow Country Park
52 Hill Top Farm
53 Valehouse Reservoir
54 Cote Lodge
55 Longbarn Pond
56 Grey Mist Mere
57 Ackers Pit
58 Moore Quarry
59 Appleton Reservoir
60 Grimsditch Mill Pool
61 Whitley Pool
62 Budworth Mere
63 Pickmere
64 Lymm Dam
65 Wetgate Pool
66 Abbey Village Top Lodge
67 Tatton Mere
68 Tabley Mere
69 Black Lake
70 Mobberly Pool
71 Moss Pool
72 Fryers Moss
73 Astle Pool
74 Capesthorne Hall
75 Chain and Gate Pool
76 Poynton Pool
77 Wide Hole
78 Teggsnose Reservoir
79 Errwood Reservoir
80 Sandiway Lake
81 Petty Pool
82 Rookery Pool
83 New Pool
84 Dale Green Coarse Fishery
85 Newbridge Pool
86 Oulton Mill Pool
87 Billinge Green
88 Pritchards Pits
89 Shakerley Mere
90 Goostrey Pool
91 Orchard Pool
92 Sandybank Pool
93 Hurleston Reservoir
94 Sandhole
95 Clough Hall Lake

Southern Area Still Waters

Abney Park Lake

Cheadle
Stockport Leisure Services
Roach, Bream, Tench, Perch, Pike, Carp
Ease of access for disabled anglers, ambulant and non-ambulant.
This water is free, but anglers must hold a current NRA licence

Ackers Pit

Stockton Heath
Warrington Anglers Association
Medium sized lake containing *Carp, Roach, Bream, Tench*
Ease of access for disabled anglers, ambulant and non-ambulant.
Annual Permit

Alexandra Park Lake

Moss Side, Manchester
Manchester Recreational Services Department
Freshwater fish
Ease of access for disabled anglers, ambulant and non-ambulant.
Day ticket/Annual permit

Appleton Reservoir

Higher Walton
Warrington Anglers Association
Medium sized lake containing *Trout*
Fly Fishing only
Annual permit

Arrowe Park

Birkenhead
Association of Wirral Angling Clubs
Roach, Bream, Rudd, Tench, Carp, Perch, Crucian Carp
Day Ticket

Astle Pool

Chelford
Warrington Anglers Association
5 acre lake containing *Bream, Tench, Mirror & Common Carp, Roach, Perch, Pike*
Limited access for ambulant disabled.
Annual permit

Billinge Green

Nr Leftwich
Northwich Anglers Association
Medium sized lake containing *Common & Mirror Carp, Tench, Bream, Rudd, Roach, Pike, Perch*
Ease of access for disabled anglers, ambulant and non-ambulant. There is a purpose built platform which will accommodate wheelchairs, and a ramp leading on to it.
Annual permit

Black Lake

Lindow Common, Wilmslow
Macclesfield Leisure Services
Freshwater fish
Ease of access for disabled anglers, ambulant and non-ambulant.
Annual permit

Boggart Hole Clough Lake

Blackley, Manchester
Manchester Recreational Services Department
Roach, Carp
Ease of access for disabled anglers, ambulant and non-ambulant. This venue is also suitable for blind anglers, if accompanied. Written permission is needed prior to fishing to enable vehicles to go to the lake.
Day ticket/Annual permit

Bold Pool

Bold, St Helens
Warrington Anglers Association
Small pool containing *Roach, Rudd, Tench, Perch*
Annual permit

Budworth Mere

Great Budworth
Joint control by Warrington Anglers Association, and Northwich Anglers Association
Large mere containing *Bream, Roach, Perch, Tench, Pike*
Annual permit

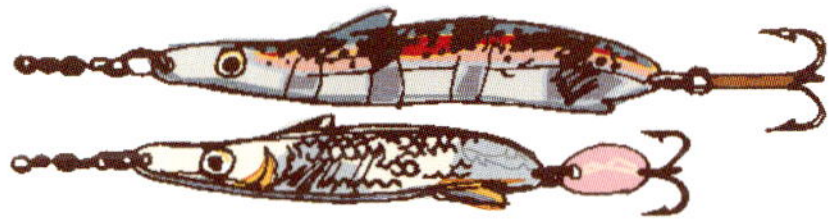

Canal Pit

Nr Leftwich
Northwich Anglers Association
Common & Mirror Carp, Tench, Roach, Rudd, Perch
Annual Permit

Capesthorne Hall

Capesthorne Estate, Nr Chelford
Stoke-on-Trent Angling Society
Two pools, eight acres in size, containing *Pike, Bream, Tench, Roach, Rudd, Crucian Carp*
Ease of access for disabled anglers, ambulant and non-ambulant.
Annual permit/Guest permit if accompanied by a member of the Society

Captains Pit

Wallasey
Association of Wirral Anglers Club
Roach, Rudd, Tench, Bream, Carp, Perch, Crucian Carp
Day ticket/Annual Permit

Carr Mill Dam

St Helens Angling Association
A large dam containing *Roach, Bream, Tench, Carp, Perch*
Match venue
Annual permit

Castle Pits

Sandbach
Congleton Anglers Society
Carp, Roach, Tench, Perch
Ease of access for ambulant disabled anglers only.
Annual permit

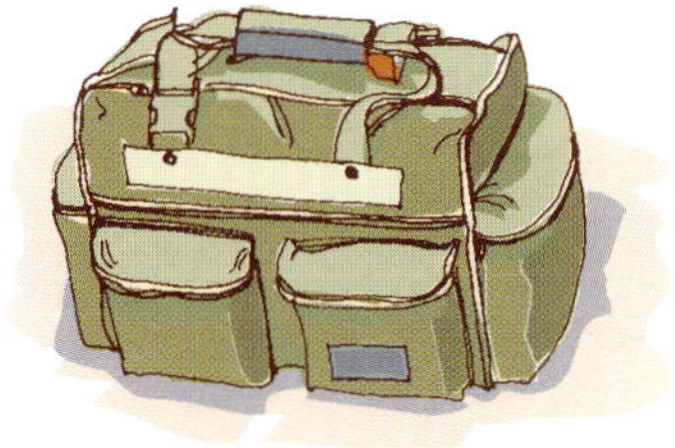

Castle Pool

Bolesworth Castle Estate,
Tattenhall, Nr Chester
Stoke-on-Trent Angling Society
Eight acre lake containing *Carp, Bream, Tench, Crucian Carp, Roach*
Annual permit/Guest permit if accompanied by member of the Society

Central Park

Wallasey
Association of Wirral Angling Clubs
Roach, Crucian Carp, Rudd, Bream, Tench, Carp, Perch
Day Ticket/Annual permit

Chain and Gate Pool

Gawsworth
Macclesfield Waltonians Angling Society
Carp, Tench, Roach, Rudd
Annual permit

Chorlton Water Park

Chorlton, Manchester
Mersey Valley Countryside Warden Service
Carp, Pike, Roach, Tench, Perch, Chub, Rudd, Crucian Carp
Keep-nets are not allowed
Ease of access for disabled anglers, ambulant and non-ambulant.
Day ticket

Cicely Mill Pool

Bucklow Hill
Warrington Anglers Association
Medium sized lake containing *Bream, Roach, Perch, Tench, Common & Mirror Carp, Pike*
Ease of access for ambulant disabled anglers.
Annual permit

Claredon New Water

Bury District Angling Society
Bream, Tench, Roach, Pike, Perch, Carp
Annual permit

Clarence Park Lido

Bury
Ramsbottom Angling Association
Bream, Tench, Roach, Pike, Perch, Carp
No fishing on Wednesdays or Sundays.
Ease of access disabled anglers, ambulant and non-amulant.
Annual permit, but permit holders may take a guest

Clifton Marina

Swinton
Salford-inter Angling Association
Roach, Bream, Carp, Grass Carp, Pike, Tench, Crucian Carp
Disabled platforms.
Car parking 1/4 mile from water.
Match Venue, 60 pegs
Day ticket

Clough Hall Lake

Kidsgrove and District Angling Association
Roach, Rudd, Bream, Carp, Tench
Annual permit

Clowbridge Reservoir

Rossendale
North West Water Ltd,
Mr P. Luff, Access and Recreation Manager
Freshwater fish, Trout
Limited access for disabled anglers.
Day ticket

Clowes Park

Higher Broughton
Salford-inter Angling Association
Roach, Crucian Carp, Tench, Perch
Ease of access for ambulant disabled anglers only.
Day ticket

Cobblers Gorse

Antrobus
Lymm Angling Club
Small pool containing *Trout*
Fly Fishing only
Annual permit

Coffin Lodge

Tottington
Bury District Angling Society
Bream, Tench, Roach, Carp, Pike, Perch
Ease of access for disabled anglers, ambulant and non-ambulant.
Annual Permit

Compstall Lodge

Etherow Country Park
Stockport and District Anglers Federation
Bream, Roach, Carp, Tench, Pike, Perch
Ease of access for disabled anglers, ambulant and non-ambulant.
Toilet Facilities
Annual permit

Cote Lodge

Glossop, Derbyshire
North West Water Ltd,
Mr G. Grimes,
Recreation and Conservation Officer
Telephone (0161) 480 6271
Trout
Day ticket

Cromptons

Bury District Angling Society
Bream, Tench, Carp, Roach, Pike, Perch
Day ticket with member of club only

Dale Green Coarse Fishery

Mr & Mrs Harding,
Dale Green Farm, Marton,
Winsford, Cheshire
Four acre lake containing *Carp, Roach, Bream, Tench, Pike, Perch*
Ease of access for ambulant disabled anglers. There are two pegs for wheelchairs by prior arrangement.
Day ticket

Dam Head Lodge Reservoir

Prestwich and Whitefield Angling Club
2 1/2 acre reservoir containing *Tench, Carp, Roach*
Ease of access for ambulant disabled anglers, and non-ambulant anglers if prior notice is given.
Day ticket/Annual Permit

Debdale Lower Reservoir

Debdale Park, Gorton
Manchester Recreational Services Department
Roach, Perch, Carp, Tench, Bream, Trout
Ease of access for disabled anglers, ambulant and non-ambulant. This venue is also suitable for blind anglers if accompanied.
No keepnets or ground baits/cereal baits allowed.
Day ticket

Dig-Pit

Carr Mill
St Helens Angling Association
Medium sized pool containing *Roach, Tench, Carp, Bream, Perch*
Annual permit

Double Woods Pool

Mere Corner, Knutsford
Altrincham and District Angling Club
Roach, Carp, Tench, Bream, Pike, Perch
Ease of access for disabled anglers, ambulant and non-ambulant. Wheelchair anglers may need assistance.
Day Ticket with member of club only/Annual permit

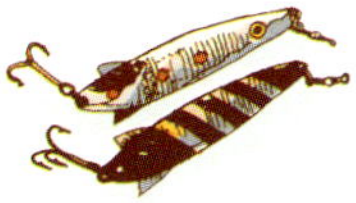

Drinkwater Park Lake

Agecroft, Bolton
Stockport and District Anglers Federation
Freshwater Fish
Very limited access for disabled anglers.
Annual permit

Dukes Pool

Nr Sandbach
Lymm Anglers Club
A small pool containing *Carp, Crucian Carp, Roach, Rudd*
No carbon rods or poles to be used on this water, due to overhead power lines.
Annual permit

Endcrofts Pond

Ramsbottom Angling Association
Bream, Roach, Tench, Perch, Pike, Carp
Ease of access for disabled anglers, ambulant and non-amulant.
Annual permit, permit holders may take a guest

Errwood Reservoir

North West Water Ltd
Mr P. Luff,
Recreation and Conservation Manager,
Telephone (01204) 696118
Trout
Ease of access for ambulant disabled anglers. There are a number of wheelchair routes and activities.
Toilet facilities
Day ticket

Etherow Country Park

Stockport and District Anglers Federation
Carp, Tench, Bream, Roach, Perch, Pike
Ease of access for disabled anglers, ambulant and non-ambulant
Day ticket available from Etherow/Goyt Valley Warden Service. Annual permits from Stockport and District Anglers Federation

Fir Tree Flash

Leigh
Fir Tree Angling Society
Roach, Perch, Bream, Tench, Pike
Ease of access for disabled anglers, ambulant and non-ambulant. Wheelchair users will need assistance.
Day ticket/Annual permit

Founders Pool

Antrobus
Lymm Angling Club
One acre in size, containing *Carp, Roach, Rudd, Perch*
Ease of access for ambulant disabled anglers.
Annual permit

Fryers Moss

Fryers Moss Lane, Knutsford
South Manchester Angling Club
Roach, Perch, Tench, Rudd, Bream, Carp
Ease of access for ambulant disabled anglers.
Restricted and Annual permit

Gigg Lane Paper Waters

Bury and District Angling Society
Freshwater fish
Ease of access for disabled anglers, ambulant and non-ambulant.
Day ticket with member of club only/Annual permit

Goostrey Pool

Congleton Anglers Society
Roach, Carp, Tench, Bream
Limited access for ambulant disabled anglers.
Annual permit

Gorse Pool

Antrobus
Lymm Angling Club
Chub, Dace, Silver Orfe, ornamental species of fish
Ease of access for disabled anglers, ambulant and non-ambulant.
Annual permit

Gorton Reservoir

Denton Arm, Greater Manchester
North West Water Ltd
Mr G. Grimes,
Conservation and Recreation Manager
Telephone (0161) 480 6271
Freshwater fish
Ease of access for disabled anglers, ambulant and non-ambulant.
Day ticket

Gorton Upper Reservoir

'Lawrence Scott Arm' Manchester City Council, Recreational Services Department
Carp, Roach, Tench, Bream, Perch, Pike
Ease of access for disabled anglers, ambulant and non-ambulant.
Day ticket

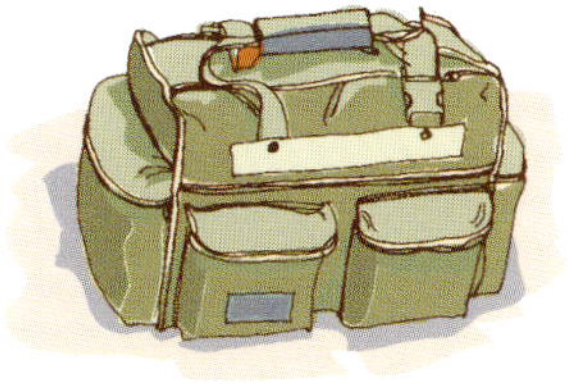

Grey Mist Mere

Woolston, Warrington
Warrington Anglers Association
A large mere containing *Mirror & Common Carp, Roach, Perch, Tench, Crucian Carp, Pike.*
Trout are stocked in the close season for fly fishing only.
Ease of access for disabled anglers, ambulant and non-ambulant.
Annual permit

Grimsditch Mill Pool

Norcott Brook, Nr Warrington
Lymm Angling Club
Carp fishery, Ornamental fish, Wels Catfish
Ease of access for ambulant disabled anglers.
Annual permit

Grove Lodge

Littleborough
Todmorden Angling Society
Mixed fishery
Open all year round
Annual permit

Harthill

Bolesworth Castle Estate, Tattenhall
Stoke-on-Trent Angling Society
5 acre lake containing *Wild Carp, Tench, Roach, Rudd, Eels*
Annual permit

Hazel Hall Lane

Ramsbottom Angling Association
Bream, Tench, Roach, Pike, Perch, Carp
Ease of access for disabled anglers, ambulant and non-ambulant.
Drivers: park on the grass verge, do not obstruct access for farm vehicles.
Annual permit, permit holders may take a guest

Hill Top Farm

Mellor
Stockport and District Anglers Federation
Freshwater fish
Very limited access for disabled anglers.
Annual permit

Hollingworth Lake

Rochdale
Chief Warden,
Information Centre,
Hollingworth Lake Country Park
Roach, Tench, Rudd, Carp, Perch, Pike
Ease of access for disabled anglers, ambulant and non-ambulant.
Match bookings in advance from Visitors Centre.
Day ticket available from the bank Ranger/ Annual permits from Rochdale Council Leisure department

Horseshoe Pool

Antrobus
Lymm Angling Club
Small pool containing *Roach, Rudd, Crucian Carp, Perch, Goldfish, Tench, Carp, Ghost Carp*
Ease of access for ambulant disabled anglers.
Annual permit

Humphries Lake

Middleton
Disabled Anglers Federation
Freshwater fish
Wheelchair anglers only. Ease of access for non-ambulant disabled anglers.
Annual permit

Hurleston Reservoir

Crewe L.M.R. Angling Society.
Carp, Tench, Roach, Bream, Perch, Pike
Annual permit

Jumbles Reservoir

Bolton
North West Water Ltd
Mr P. Luff,
Recreation and Conservation Manager
Telephone (01204) 696118
Tench, Bream, Carp, Roach, Perch, Pike
Ease of access for disabled anglers, ambulant and non-ambulant.
Free fishery to NRA licence holders

King George V Pool

Altrincham
Trafford Leisure Services
Freshwater fish
Ease of access for disabled anglers, ambulant and non-ambulant.
Day ticket/Annual Permit

Kirklees Carcus

Tottington
Bury District Angling Society
Freshwater fish
Day ticket with member of club only/Annual permit

Know Mill Water

Bury and District Angling Society
Freshwater fish
Ease of access for disabled anglers, ambulant and non-ambulant.
Annual permit

Knypersley Reservoir

Cheshire Anglers Association
Roach, Rudd, Tench, Bream, Carp, Pike, Perch
Very limited accesss for disabled anglers.
Annual permit

Land Gate Lodges

Bryn
Garswood Angling Society
Roach, Carp, Tench, Bream, Pike, Perch
Ease of access for disabled anglers, ambulant and non-ambulant.
Annual permit

Leg O' Mutton Dam

St Helens Angling Association
Large lake containing *Roach, Rudd, Tench, Bream, Carp, Pike, Perch*
Annual permit

Longbarn Pond

Fearnhead, Warrington
Lymm Angling Club
Carp, Tench, Roach, Perch
Ease of access for disabled anglers, ambulant and non-ambulant, but parking difficult.
Day ticket

Long Causeway Pond

Atherton, Leigh
Lymm Angling Club
Small pool containing *Ghost Carp, Rudd, Roach, Tench, Carp, Crucian Carp.*
Ease of access for disabled anglers, ambulant and non-ambulant. Wheelchair anglers will need assistance.
Annual permit

Lower Lake

Birkenhead Park, Birkenhead
Association of Wirral Angling Clubs
Roach, Rudd, Crucian Carp, Bream, Tench, Carp, Perch
Match Fishing only
Annual permit

Lymm Dam

Lymm Angling Club
15 acre lake containing *Carp, Roach, Rudd, Tench, Bream, Pike, Chub, Barbel, Orfe*
Ease of access for disabled anglers, ambulant and non-ambulant.
Match venue
Day ticket/Annual permit

Lymmvale

Nr Whitegate
Lymm Angling Club
7 acre lake containing *Tench, Chub, Golden Orfe, Grayling, Barbel, Trout*
Ease of access for the ambulant disabled.
Annual permit

Lymmvale Stockpond

Nr Whitegate
Lymm Angling Club
Small pool containing *Tench, Carp, Golden Orfe, Grass Carp, Wels Catfish*
Annual permit

Marton Hole

Winsford and District Anglers Association
Roach, Rudd, Perch, Pike, Trout
Annual permit

Middle Place Lodges

Bryn
Garswood angling Society
Carp, Tench, Bream, Roach, Rudd, Pike, Perch
Ease of access for disabled anglers, ambulant and non-ambulant.
Annual permit

Mobberley Pool

Altrincham and District Angling Club
Roach, Rudd, Tench, Perch, Pike
Ease of access for ambulant disabled anglers.
Day ticket with member of club/Annual permit

Moore Quarry

Warrington Anglers Association
Large quarry containing *Tench, Bream, Roach, Perch, Pike*
Annual permit

Mossbank Pool

Ollerton
Lymm Angling Club
Small pool containing *Tench, Crucian Carp, Roach, Rudd, Carp*
Annual permit

Moss Pool

Ollerton
Lymm Angling Club
Small pool containing *Tench, Crucian Carp, Roach, Rudd, Carp*
Annual permit

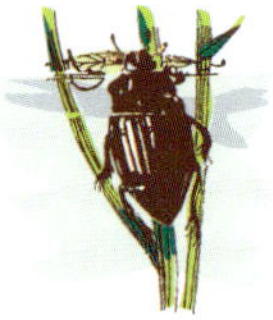

Mount Pool

Gawsworth
Macclesfield Waltonians Angling Society
Carp, Tench, Roach, Rudd
Annual permit

Newbridge Pool

Winsford and District Anglers Association
Roach, Rudd, Carp, Bream, Tench, Perch, Pike
Ease of access for disabled anglers, ambulant and non-ambulant.
Day ticket/Annual permit

New House Farm Pool

Bramhall
Stockport and District Anglers Federation
Freshwater fish
Annual permit

New Pool

Whitegate
Winsford and District Anglers Association
Carp, Bream, Roach, Rudd, Perch, Pike
Annual permit

Newsham Park Lake

West Derby
Liverpool and District Anglers Association
Freshwater fish
Ease of access for disabled anglers, ambulant and non-ambulant.
Day ticket/Annual permit

Olives Lodges

Ramsbottom Angling Association
Bream, Roach, Tench, Pike, Perch, Carp
Ease of access for disabled anglers, ambulant and non-ambulant.
Permit holders may park in Olives car park on showing their permit to the security.
Annual permit, permit holders may take a guest.

Orchard Pools

Congleton Anglers Society
Carp, Roach, Tench, Perch
Annual permit

Orrell Water Park

Wigan Leisure Services, Countryside Section
Two lakes containing *Common Carp, Tench, Roach, Bream, Perch, Gudgeon*
Ease of access for disabled anglers, ambulant and non-ambulant.
Warden on site. Fishing from 6am till sunset.
Day ticket/Annual permit

Oulton Mill Pool

Oulton Park
Tarporley Angling Club
Freshwater fish
Ease of access for disabled anglers, ambulant and non-ambulant. Also suitable for the blind if accompanied.
Annual permit

Paddock Dam

St Helens Ramblers Angling Society
Medium sized lake containing *Carp, Tench, Bream, Roach, Pike*
Ease of access for ambulant disabled anglers.
Annual permit

Parkers Elton Vale

Bury and District Angling Society
Freshwater fish
Day ticket with member of club only/Annual permit

Patience Pool

Antrobus
Lymm Angling Club
Small pool containing *Roach, Rudd, Crucian Carp, Perch, Golden Rudd, Goldfish*
Annual permit

Petty Pool

Nr Whitegate
Northwich Anglers Association
Large mere containing *Bream, Carp, Roach, Perch, Pike, Eels*
Very limited access for ambulant disabled anglers.
Annual Permit

Pickmere Lake

Northwich Anglers Association
Large lake containing *Bream, Tench, Roach, Rudd, Perch, Pike*
Limited access for ambulant disabled anglers.
Annual permit

Piethorne Reservoir

Rochdale
Oldham Fly Fishing Club
40 acre lake containing *Brown & Rainbow Trout*
Fly fishing only
Ease of access for ambulant disabled anglers.
Day ticket/Annual permit

Platt Fields Park Boating Lake

Rusholme,
Manchester Recreational Services Department
Roach, Carp, Bream
Ease of access for disabled anglers, ambulant and non-ambulant. This venue is suitable for blind anglers if accompanied.
Day ticket/Annual permit

Poynton Pool

Stockport and District Anglers Federation
Roach, Rudd, Perch, Bream, Carp, Pike
Ease of access for disabled anglers, ambulant and non-ambulant. This venue is suitable for blind anglers if accompanied.
Day ticket/Annual permit

Pritchards Pits

(4 pools)
Davenham Angling Club
Roach, Rudd, Common & Mirror Carp, Perch, Crucian Carp
Annual permit

Prudence Pool

Antrobus
Lymm Angling Club
Small pool containing *Roach, Rudd, Perch, Tench, Carp*
Annual permit

Redesmere

Capesthorne Estate, Nr Chelford
Stoke-on-Trent Angling Society
35 acre mere containing *Common & Mirror Carp, Bream, Tench, Roach, Rudd, Pike, Perch*
Limited access for ambulant disabled anglers.
Annual permit/Guest permit if accompanied by a member of the Society

Reddish Vale Pond

Tame Valley Countryside Warden Service
Carp, Tench, Bream, Roach, Perch, Pike
Ease of access for disabled anglers, ambulant and non-ambulant.
Day ticket

Rookery Pool

Whitegate
Warrington Anglers Association
Medium sized lake containing *Carp, Tench, Bream, Roach, Rudd, Perch, Pike*
Annual permit

Rose Bank Mill

Ramsbottom Angling Association
Bream, Tench, Roach, Perch, Pike, Carp.
Ease of access for disabled anglers, ambulant and non-ambulant.
Drivers should park only in the area provided.
Annual permit, permit holders may take a guest

Royden Park

Overchurch
Association of Wirral Angling Clubs
Roach, Rudd, Tench, Carp, Crucian Carp, Bream, Perch
Day ticket/Annual permit

Sale Water Park Lake

Trafford Leisure Services
Freshwater fish
No keepnets allowed
Ease of access for disabled anglers, ambulant and non-ambulant. This venue is suitable for blind anglers if accompanied.
Day ticket/Annual permit

Sand Hole Reservoir

Swinton/Walkden
Salford Angling Club, Disabled Section
Tench, Bream, Carp, Roach, Rudd
Ease of access for disabled anglers, ambulant and non-ambulant. This venue is suitable for blind anglers if accompanied. There is a purpose built footpath and four pegs for wheelchairs.
Annual permit

Sandhole

Crewe
Crewe L.M.R. Angling Society
Roach, Rudd, Carp, Tench, Bream, Perch, Pike
Annual permit

Sandiway Lake

Marton
Warrington Anglers Association
17½ acre lake containing *Roach, Bream, Tench, Chub, Crucian Carp, Gudgeon*
Although there are two lakes, only the smaller lake is to be used.
Ease of access for disabled anglers, ambulant and non-ambulant.
Annual permit

Sandybank Pool

Nr Sandbach
Lymm Angling Club
Small pool containing *Silver Orfe, Golden Rudd, Goldfish, Ghost Carp, Golden Tench, Crucian Carp*
Limited access for ambulant disabled anglers.
Annual permit

Sandy Pool

Nr Sandbach
Lymm Angling Club
Small pool containing *Carp, Tench, Bream, Chub, Roach, Rudd, Crucian Carp, Golden Rudd, Silver Orfe, Goldfish, Ghost Carp*
Limited access for ambulant disabled anglers.
Annual Permit

Sefton Park Lake

Liverpool and District Anglers Association
Roach, Perch, Bream, Carp, Rudd
Ease of access for disabled anglers, ambulant and non-ambulant. This venue is suitable for blind anglers if accompanied.

Shakerley Mere

Lymm Angling Club
17 acre mere containing *Carp, Bream, Tench, Roach, Rudd, Crucian Carp, Perch, Trout*
Ease of access for disabled anglers, ambulant and non-ambulant.
Toilet facilities
Day ticket/Annual permit

Springwood Pool

Mobberley
Congleton Anglers Society
Carp, Tench, Bream, Roach, Perch
Annual permit

Springwood Street Pool

Ramsbottom Angling Association
Freshwater fish and Trout
No Trout to be taken from this water
Ease of access for disabled anglers, ambulant and non-ambulant.
Annual permit, permit holders may take a guest

Tabley Mere

Nr Plumley
Lymm Angling Club
47 acre mere containing *Tench, Carp, Bream, Roach, Pike*
Fishing is by boat only, and only three anglers are allowed at any one time.
Annual permit

Tabley Moat

Nr Plumley
Lymm Angling Club
10 acre lake containing *Roach, Rudd, Perch, Bream, Tench, Carp*
Ease of access for disabled anglers, ambulant and non-ambulant.
Directions given by Tabley Mere staff must be adhered to exactly.
Annual permit

Tattenhall

Nr Chester
Stoke-on-Trent Angling Society
8 acre lake containing *Carp, Bream, Tench, Crucian Carp, Roach, Eels*
Ease of access for disabled anglers, ambulant and non-ambulant. There are three wheelchair pegs.
Annual permit/Day ticket if accompanied by a member of the Society

Tatton Mere

The Director, Tatton Park, Knutsford, Cheshire
A large mere containing *Perch, Pike, Roach, Tench, Carp*
Ease of access for disabled anglers, ambulant and non-ambulant. This venue is suitable for blind anglers if accompanied.
Day ticket

Taylor and Nickolsons

Bury and District Angling Society
Freshwater fish
Ease of access for ambulant disabled anglers.
Day ticket (senior only)/Annual permit

Taylors Pool

Crewe L.M.R. Angling Society
Freshwater fish
Limited access for ambulant disabled anglers.
Annual permit

Teggsnose Reservoir

Langley
Macclesfield Waltonians Angling Society
Carp, Tench, Bream, Roach, Rudd, Crucian Carp, Perch
Day ticket/Annual permit

The Pits

Antrobus
Lymm Angling Club
Small pool containing *Bream, Silver Bream, Golden & Silver Rudd, Tench*
Annual permit

The Recreation Pond

Poulton Park, Bebington
Association of Wirral Angling Clubs
Roach, Rudd, Tench, Carp, Perch, Crucian Carp, Bream
Day ticket

Three Sisters Lake

Bryn, Ashton-in-Makerfield
Wigan Metropolitan Borough Council
Common Carp, Tench, Roach, Bream, Rudd, Gudgeon
Fishing from 8.30am until dusk
Day ticket/Annual permit available from Ranger on site

Tony Bulls Pool

Crewe L.M.R. Angling Society
Freshwater fish
Annual permit

Top Pool

Capesthorne Estate, Nr Chelford
Stoke-on-Trent Angling Society
Four acre lake containing *Bream, Tench, Carp, Roach*
Annual permit/Guest permit if accompanied by member of the Society

Top & Bottom Waters

Middleton
King William lV Newton Angling Society
Freshwater Fish
Ease of access for disabled anglers, ambulant and non-ambulant on the Bottom Water.
Parking is by the waterside.
Annual permit

Two Brooks

Ramsbottom Angling Association
Bream, Tench, Roach, Perch, Pike, Carp
Ease of access for disabled anglers, ambulant and non-ambulant.
Drivers must not obstruct access for farm vehicles.
Annual permit, permit holders may take a guest

Valehouse Reservoir

Nr Tintwistle
The Longdendale Fly Fishing Association
Trout
Fly fishing only
Ease of access for ambulant disabled anglers, part of the reservoir is suitable for wheelchairs.
Toilet facilities
Day ticket/Annual permit

Village Pool

Whitley
Lymm Angling Club
Medium sized pool containing *Carp, Roach, Tench, Bream, Rudd, Crucian Carp, Perch*
Annual permit

Walton Hall Park Lake

Liverpool and District Anglers Association
Freshwater fish
Ease of access for disabled anglers, ambulant and non-ambulant. This venue is also suitable for blind anglers.
Day ticket

Watergrove Reservoir

Rochdale
North West Water,
Warden Office
Telephone (01706) 379060
Ease of access for disabled anglers, ambulant and non-ambulant.
Parking & toilet at Windsurfing Club House/ Wardens office.
Day ticket/Permit from the on-site Warden, or Hollingworth Lake Visitor Centre

Wayoh Reservoir

Entwistle, Nr Bolton
Northern Anglers Association
Trout, Freshwater fish
Annual permit

Wetgate Pool

Nr Oughtrington
Lymm Angling Club
Small pool containing *Carp, Crucian Carp, Roach, Rudd, Tench*
Only four anglers at one time allowed.
Annual permit

Widdows Flash

Spring View
Nor-West Disabled Anglers Association
Carp, Bream, Roach, Tench, Perch, Pike
Ease of access for disabled anglers, ambulant and non-ambulant. Wheelchair pegs and parking close to water. Disabled anglers only.
Day ticket/Annual permit

Wide Hole

Higher Poynton
Northern Anglers Association
Carp, Bream, Tench, Roach, Perch, Pike
Annual permit

Whitley Pool

Frodsham District Angling Club
Freshwater fish
Annual permit

Woodbank Park Pool

Offerton
Stockport and District Anglers Federation
Freshwater fish
Very limited access for disabled anglers
Annual permit

Southern Area Rivers

River Bollin

Lymm Angling Club have four stretches of the River as follows:
Wetgate length - 2000 yards
The Mill length - 650 yards
Cinder length - 600 yards
Reddish length - 1000 yards
Roach, Barbel, Chub, Dace, Grayling, Bream, Perch, Trout, Orfe
There is limited access for ambulant disabled anglers.
Annual permit

River Bollin

Heatley
Altrincham and District Angling Club
Roach, Bream, Chub, Perch, Eels, Gudgeon
There is limited access for ambulant disabled anglers
Day ticket if accompanied by a member of the club/Annual permit

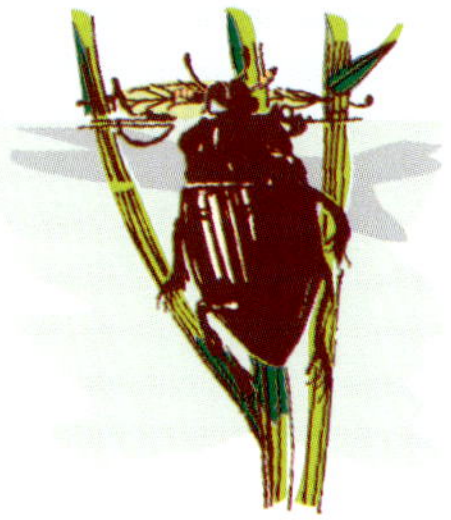

River Bollin

Bowdon
Warrington Anglers Association
Chub, Dace, Perch, Trout
Annual permit

River Dane

Lymm Angling Club
Lymm have two stretches on this river:
Manor Farm, Nr Middlewich - 600 yards
Daisybank Farm, Nr Northwich - 600 yards
Chub, Barbel, Trout, Roach, Dace, Eels, Gudgeon
Day ticket/Annual permit

River Dane

Northwich Anglers Association
This Association has four stretches of the river between Northwich and Leftwich
Chub, Roach, Bream, Carp, Barbel
There is ease of access for ambulant disabled anglers on the town centre stretch.
Annual permit

River Dane

Davenham Angling Club and Northwich Angling Association have joint control over two stretches of the River:
Victoria Bridge, Northwich to the Railway Viaduct
Spibeys, Rudheath to the no match fishing sign.
These stretches of the River are for pleasure fishing only, but have a limited ease of access for disabled anglers.
Chub, Barbel, Roach, Perch, Rainbow Trout
Annual permit

River Dane

Leftwich to Davenham
Davenham Angling Club
Chub, Barbel, Roach, Rainbow Trout
This stretch is used for match fishing at weekends.
Annual permit

River Dane

Middlewich,
Bulls Wood to Davenham village - 5 miles
Davenham Angling Club
Trout only from 1st April to 30th September
Annual Trout permit

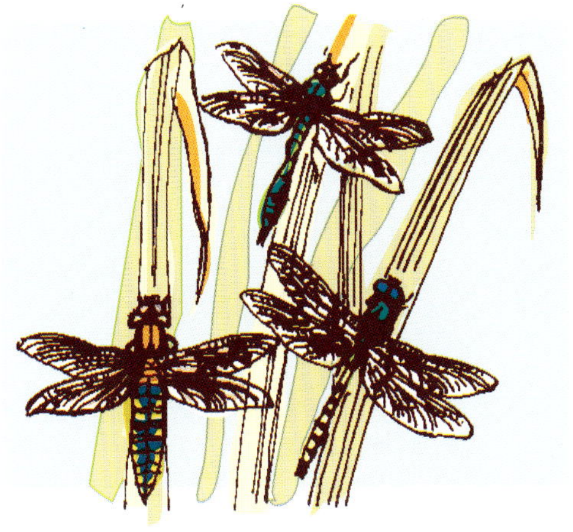

River Dane

Nr Winsford
Winsford and District Anglers Association
Chub, Barbel, Roach, Dace, Gudgeon, Trout
Day ticket/Annual permit

River Dane

1.5 miles, Holmes Chapel
Warrington Anglers Association
Roach, Perch, Trout, Gudgeon
Limited access for ambulant disabled anglers.
Annual permit

River Dane

Town Stretch and Forge Lane, Congleton
Congleton Anglers Society
Chub, Barbel, Dace, Roach, Pike, Perch, Trout
Ease of access for disabled anglers, ambulant and non-ambulant.
Annual permit

River Dane

Congleton Anglers Society
The society has a further three stretches of the river they are:
Swettenham,
Somerford Park,
Radnor
Chub, Barbel, Dace, Roach, Pike, Perch, Trout
There is limited access for ambulant disabled anglers.
Annual permit

River Etherow

Compstall Stockport (downstream from bridge to Redbrow Wood)
Compstall Angling Club
Freshwater fish
Annual permit

River Gowy

Downstream of Bridge Trafford - 2 miles
Warrington Anglers Association
Both banks can be fished from, except for the stretch near the bridge which is left bank only fishing.
Annual permit

River Goyt

Marple
Stockport and District Anglers Federation
Chub, Dace, Roach, Perch, Pike
Day ticket/Annual permit

River Mersey

Warrington Anglers Association
There are two stretches of the river adjacent to Knutsford Road, Warrington and Kingsway, Warrington
Roach, Bream, Carp
Ease of access for disabled anglers, ambulant and non-ambulant, near Kingsway. Wheelchair anglers will need assistance.
Barbless hooks only to be used. No keepnets unless in matches.
Annual Permit

Peover Eye,

Withington Green
Lymm Angling Club
Downstream of the mill, for one field left hand bank
Rainbow & Brown Trout, Grayling, Chub, Dace
Ease of access for ambulant disabled anglers.
Barbless hooks compulsory, and catch returns.
This fishery is affected by overhead electric powerlines.
Annual Permit

River Weaver

7 miles from Winsford to Saltersford Locks
Northwich Angling Association
Common Carp, Crucian Carp, Chub, Bream, Tench, Roach, Rudd, Dace, Pike, Perch, Eels
Ease of access for disabled anglers, ambulant and non-ambulant, in the Northwich Town Centre there is limited access at Lock Street, Vale Royal and Hartford Bridge.
Annual Permit

River Weaver

Winsford and District Anglers Association
Roach, Tench, Bream, Carp, Chub, Perch, Pike
Ease of access for disabled anglers, ambulant and non-ambulant.
Day ticket/Annual permit

River Weaver

Nantwich Angling Society and Wych Anglers have control from 1 mile below Nantwich to 4 miles above Nantwich
Roach, Rudd, Bream, Carp, Tench, Pike, Perch
Ease of access for disabled anglers, ambulant and non-ambulant, in Nantwich for approximately 1 mile.
Annual permit

River Weaver

Vale Royal
Northern Anglers Association
Chub, Bream, Carp, Tench, Perch, Pike
Subscription for affiliated clubs and individuals

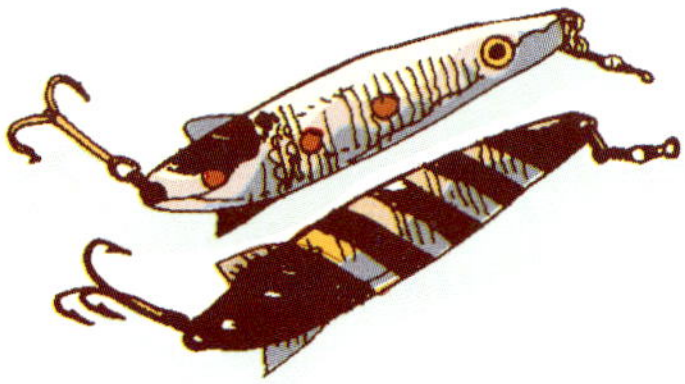

River Weaver

Wrenbury
Nantwich Angling Society
Bream, Roach, Carp, Tench, Pike
Annual permit

River Weaver

Batherton
Crewe L.M.R. Angling Society
Roach, Dace, Chub, Trout, Gudgeon
Annual permit

Wincham Brook

800 yards, Plumley
Lymm Angling Club
Roach, Chub, Barbel, Grayling, Perch, Gudgeon, Trout
Annual permit

Wincham Brook

Lostock Gralam
Northwich Anglers Association
Chub, Dace, Roach, Gudgeon, Trout
Annual permit

Canals

Ashton Canal

3 miles
British Waterways
Manchester to Fairfield Locks, Nr Droylsden, Except Bridge 10 to 11
Roach, Carp, Tench, Bream
Ease of access for disabled anglers, ambulant and non-ambulant.
All of this canal stretch may be booked for matches.
Day ticket/Monthly permit/Annual permit

Ashton Canal

Portland Basin Heritage Centre,
Tame Valley Countryside Warden Service
Roach, Perch, Carp, Tench
Ease of access for disabled anglers, ambulant and non-ambulant. This stretch of the canal is suitable for blind anglers if accompanied.
Day ticket

Bolton Canal

Bolton Jubilee Disabled Club
Roach, Carp, Tench, Roach, Bream
Ease of access for disabled anglers, ambulant and non-ambulant.
Day ticket/Annual permit

Bridgewater Canal

From Broadheath Bridge Timperley up to Town Bridge, and the Trafford Arm
Northern Anglers Association
Roach, Bream, Carp, Tench, Pike, Perch
Ease of access for disabled anglers, ambulant and non-ambulant.
Subscription for affiliated clubs and individuals

Bridgewater Canal

16 miles
Warrington Anglers Association
Roach, Tench, Carp, Bream, Pike, Perch, Trout
Warrington A.A. control from Preston Brook Tunnel to Broadheath, Nr Lymm.
Ease of access for disabled anglers, ambulant and non-ambulant. There is a car park and a ramp onto the tow-path to facilitate wheelchairs at Pickerings Bridge, Thelwall, but there are many areas that have access throughout the 16 miles of canal.
Annual permit

Lancaster Canal

From Preston to Tewitfields on the main line and Glasson Arm, plus a stretch at Stainton
Northern Anglers Association
Roach, Carp, Tench, Bream, Pike, Perch
Ease of access for disabled anglers, ambulant and non-ambulant.
Subscription for affiliated clubs and individual

Leeds and Liverpool Canal

From Riley Green to Hapton
Hyndburn and Blackburn Angling Association
Roach, Tench, Carp, Bream, Perch
Ease of access for disabled anglers, ambulant and non-ambulant.
Day ticket/Annual permit

Leeds and Liverpool Canal

From the bottom of Johnstons Hill Lock Chorley to Long Inge Bridge
Northern Anglers Association
Roach, Tench, Carp, Bream, Perch
Ease of access for disabled anglers, ambulant and non-ambulant.
Subscription for affiliated clubs and individuals

Leeds and Liverpool Canal

From Saracens Head, Halsall to Liverpool City
Liverpool District Anglers Association
Roach, Rudd, Tench, Perch, Carp, Pike
Ease of access for disabled anglers, ambulant and non-ambulant.
Day ticket/Annual permit

Llangollen Canal

45 miles
British Waterways
Between Hurleston and Llangollen
Roach, Perch, Bream, Tench, Carp
Monthly permits only (this fishery is only partly in the North West Region)

Llangollen Canal

2 miles
Bridge 16, Wrenbury to Bridge 22, Thomasons
Cheshire Anglers Association
Roach, Tench, Bream, Carp, Pike, Perch
Ease of access for disabled anglers, ambulant and non-ambulant.
Annual permit/Subscription for affiliated clubs

Macclesfield Canal

Buglawton
Macclesfield Waltonians Angling Society
Bream, Roach, Rudd, Tench, Carp, Perch, Pike
Ease of access for disabled anglers, ambulant and non-ambulant.
Match venue
Annual permit

Macclesfield Canal

From Marple Top Lock to Buxton Road Bridge
Northern Anglers Association
Roach, Carp, Tench, Bream, Pike, Perch
Ease of access for disabled anglers, ambulant and non-ambulant.
Subscription for affiliated clubs and individuals

Macclesfield Canal

Kidsgrove and District Angling Association
Roach, Bream, Carp, Tench, Pike, Perch
Ease of access for disabled anglers, ambulant and non-ambulant.
Annual Permit

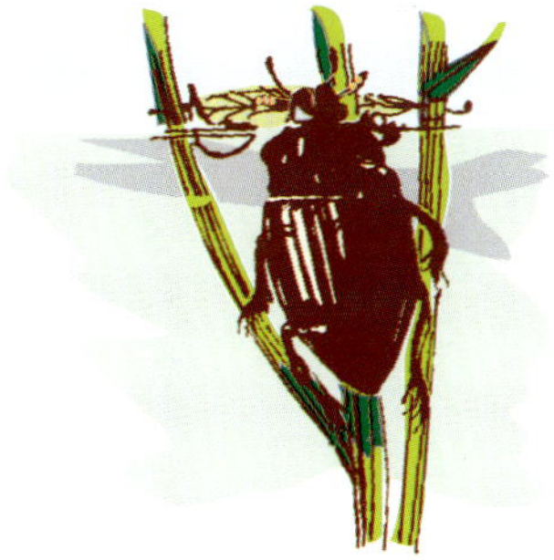

Macclesfield Canal

Congleton Anglers Association
Roach, Bream, Tench, Pike, Perch
Ease of access for disabled anglers, ambulant and non-ambulant.
Day ticket/Annual permit

Old Quay Canal

Warrington
Lymm Angling Club
Roach, Carp, Golden Rudd, Perch, Crucian Carp
Ease of access for disabled anglers, ambulant and non-ambulant.
This fishery is affected by overhead electric powerlines.
Day ticket/Annual

Rochdale Canal

Stockport and District Anglers Federation control two stretches:
Slattocks Bridge to Stake Hill Industrial Estate
Poplar Street to Failsworth
Roach, Bream, Carp, Tench, Pike, Perch
There is limited access for disabled anglers.

Rufford Canal

Liverpool and District Anglers Association
Roach, Carp, Tench, Bream, Pike, Perch
Ease of access for disabled anglers, ambulant and non-ambulant.
Day ticket/Annual permit

Sankey and St Helens Canal

Widnes
Lymm Angling Club
Carp, Bream, Roach, Rudd, Perch, Goldfish, Ghost Carp, Shubunkins, Eels
Limited access for ambulant disabled anglers.
Day ticket/Annual permit

Sankey & St Helens Canal

Warrington
Lymm Angling Club
This fishery is made up of two parts:
Phase 1. Runs from Callands Pool to Old Warrington Road.
Phase 2. Runs from Old Liverpool Road to Fiddlers Ferry.
Both of these stretches have ease of access for disabled anglers, ambulant and non-ambulant. If there are any difficulties the Warrington Borough Council Park Rangers, who are on duty on Phase 1, will lend assistance to disabled anglers.

Sankey & St Helens Canal

Newton-le-Willows Anglers Association
Roach, Tench, Carp, Bream, Chub, Pike, Perch
Ease of access for disabled anglers, ambulant and non-ambulant.
Day ticket/Annual permit

Sankey & St Helens Canal

St Helens Angling Association
Roach, Tench, Bream, Carp, Pike, Perch
Ease of access for disabled anglers, ambulant and non-ambulant.
Annual permit

Shropshire Union Canal

40 miles
From Audlem Locks to Ellesmere Port including the Middlewich Branch
British Waterways
Roach, Carp, Tench, Bream, Pike, Perch
Ease of access for disabled anglers, ambulant and non-ambulant.
Day ticket/Monthly permit/Annual permit

Shropshire Union Canal

9 miles
Bridge 60 Tyrley Locks to Audlem Bottom Lock Bridge 15
Cheshire Anglers Association
Roach, Tench, Bream, Carp, Perch, Pike
Ease of access for disabled anglers, ambulant and non-ambulant.
Annual permit/Subscription for affiliated clubs

Trent and Mersey Canal

7 miles
Cheshire Anglers Association
Cheshire AA have two stretches on this canal:
Bridge 141 Rode Heath to Bridge 159 Rookery
Elworth Boothlane Locks to the junction of the Shropshire Union Canal at Middlewich
Roach, Tench, Carp, Bream, Pike, Perch
Ease of access for disabled anglers, ambulant and non-ambulant.
Annual permit/Subscription for affiliated clubs

Trent and Mersey Canal

Kidsgrove and District Angling Association
Roach, Carp, Tench, Bream Perch
Ease of access for disabled anglers, ambulant and non-ambulant.
Annual permit

Trent and Mersey Canal

Warrington Angling Association and Northwich Angling Association jointly control 15 miles of the canal, from Preston Brook Tunnel to Northwich Town Centre
Roach, Carp, Tench, Pike, Perch, Bream
Ease of access for disabled anglers, ambulant and non-ambulant.
Annual permit

Upper and Lower Peak Forest Canal

Stockport and District Anglers Federation
Roach, Bream, Tench, Perch, Pike
There is limited access for disabled anglers.
Annual permit

Addresses & Information

When making inquiries to the secretaries of the angling organisations listed below, it is advised that contact be made by post with a stamped addressed envelope for a reply.

Accrington and District Fishing Club

The Secretary Mr Alan Balderstone,
42 Townley Avenue,
Huncoat, Accrington
Disabled anglers who have been a member for three years may receive concessionary prices for annual permits on proof of disability. Haggs Reservoir has a pier for the use of disabled anglers.

Anglers Co-operative Association

The ACA was founded in 1948 to use common law to obtain injunctions to prevent further pollution and to obtain damages, and it has been doing this with great success right up to the present. If you wish to support the 'Get Fresh' campaign and to join the ACA please write for a leaflet from:
Mr Allen Edwards ACA
23 Castlegate
Grantham
Lincs, NG31 6SW

Association of Wirral Angling Clubs

The Chairman Mr D.E. Billing
2 Patterdale Road
Bebington
Wirral
Merseyside, L63 3BN
The Association has six clubs affiliated to it, and gives concessionary permits to disabled anglers on proof of disability. It is hoped that two disabled pegs will be made at the Birkenhead Park (Upper) so that they may participate in matches.

Altrincham and District Angling Club

The Hon/Sec Mr D. Cooper
34 Clarke Crescent
Hale
Altrincham
Altrincham DAC allows concessionary permits to disabled anglers on proof of disability, which is at the committee's discretion.

Ashton Centre NAA

The Secretary Mr A.G.R. Brown
10 Dale Road
Golborne
Warrington

Barns Fold Fishery

Mr F. Casson
Barns Fold Lane
Goosnargh
Nr Preston
There are platforms for wheelchairs, and a wheelchair boat is planned. There are parking and toilet facilities.

Bentham Angling Association

The Secretary Mr E. Holt
13 Springfield Crescent
High Bentham

Blackburn Centre NAA

The Secretary Mr D. Isherwood
51 Brighton Terrace
Darwen
This centre has three other clubs within the area.

Bollington & Royal Oak Angling Society

The Secretary Mr Brocklehurst
5 Greenbank Drive
Bollington
Macclesfield
Cheshire, SK10 5LW
The society has created two wheelchair pegs which are situated on Lowerhouse Pool. The society is very supportive with reference to disabled anglers, and gives concessionary permits on proof of disability.

Bolton Centre NAA
The Secretary Mr T.A. McKee
1 Lever Edge Road
Bolton

Bolton Jubilee Disabled Club
The Hon/Sec Mr A. Broughton
1 Long Den Street
Bolton
Lancs, BLl 4HT
All disabled anglers are welcome, both ambulant and non-ambulant.

Bowland Game-Fishing Association
The Secretary Mr B. Hoggarth
1 Moorfield Road
Leyland
Preston
Lancs, PR5 3AR
Only Parsonage Reservoir is a day ticket water, and tickets are available from Roe Lee Tackle Box, Blackburn.

Brampton Angling Association
The Secretary Mr T. Donockley
1 Denton Crescent
Low Row
Brampton, Cumbria
All waters are in the East and North Cumbria, 14 miles from Carlisle.

British Waterways, North West
Regional Manager Mr D. Cochrane
British Waterways
Navigation Road
Northwich
Cheshire, CW8 lBH
Telephone (01606) 74321
Fax (01606) 871471

Briarcroft Fisheries
Mr P. Ashcroft
Briarcroft
Rawcliffe Road
St Michaels
There are parking and toilet facilities. Food and fishing bait is available.

Burnley Centre NAA
The Secretary Mr Furness
26 Grassington Drive
Burnley

Bury and District Angling Society
The Secretary Mr F. Booth
142 Bury Road
Tottington
Nr Bury
Lancs, BL8 3DX
No keepnets are allowed on Coffin Lodge Lake, and no Carp or Tench are to be retained in keepnets on any of the society's waters, except in matches. Wheelchair anglers have priority on stillage pegs, able-bodied anglers must give up these pegs if requested to by wheelchair anglers. A key to the waters can be obtained from the Secretary and local tackle shops.

Calder Vale Centre, Burnley NAA
The Secretary Mr E. Shaw
9 Melbourne Street
Padiham
Burnley, BB12 7EU

Carlisle Angling Association
The Secretary Mr A. Jones
10 Jackson Street
Carlisle, CAl 2BD
Annual permit, day and weekly permits; a waiting list exsists for Annual permits. The association has a number of ambulant members, but the waters are not suitable for non-ambulant anglers.

Carnforth and District Anglers Association
The Secretary Mr A. McCartney
3 Ullswater Crescent
Carnforth
Lancashire, LA5 9AY
Annual permit, day or weekly permits can be obtained from:
Mr I.K. McCartney
20 Coniston Road
Carnforth
Lancs, LA5 9AZ
Holmere Tarn is winter fly fishing only.

Cheshire Anglers Association

The Hon/Sec Mr G. Brassington
12 Highfield Drive
Nantwich
Cheshire
Cheshire AA gives concessionary rates for permits on proof of disability and encourages disabled anglers. This association is made up of 40 affiliated angling clubs, who retain their own waters. If any angler wishes to join a club within an area they should contact the Secretary in question (see addresses).

Coldwell Inn Activities Centre

Back Lane
Southfield
Burnley, BB10 3RG
This is a registered charity.
Coldwell Inn is a residental/day centre, which provides facilities and activities for a wide range of handicapped users. The centre offers full board for 16 visitors and self-catering for 21 visitors, and rooms are available for daily hire. There are a large number of activities ranging from horse riding, which is for handicapped groups only, to archery, craft work and fishing which is day ticket and is available to all, but they must have a NRA Rod Licence and a permit. For further details of activities and information, please contact the Manager.

Compstall Angling Club

The Secretary Mr B.P. Bennett
74 Dialstone Lane
Offerton
Stockport, SK2 6AQ

Congleton Anglers Society

The Secretary Mr N.J. Bours
8 Norfolk Road
Congleton
There are purpose built disabled pegs situated on Goodwins Pool, and large sized pegs on Springwood Pool. The society gives concessionary rates to the disabled on proof of disability, and at the committee's discretion. Fishing all year round but no keepnets are to be used on the River Dane between 15th March and 16th June.
Guest tickets are available, but guests must be accompanied by a current member of the society.

Coppenhall WMC

(Affiliated member of Cheshire AA)
The Secretary
Coppenhall WMC
North Street
Crewe

Crewe Amalgamated Anglers

(Affiliated member of Cheshire AA)
The Secretary Mr Oakes
Beech Street
Crewe

Crewe LMR Angling Society

(Affiliated member of Cheshire AA)
The Chairman Mr M. Harding
Cubicle Shop
BREL
West Street
Crewe

Crewe Pioneer Anglers

(Affiliated member of Cheshire AA)
The Secretary Mr W. Hart
Pioneer Anglers Club
Underwood Lane
Crewe

Crewe Post Office AC

(Affiliated member of Cheshire AA)
The Secretary Mr B.D. Gregory
56 Westbourne Avenue
Crewe

Crewe Welcome Club
(Affiliated member of Cheshire AA)
The Secretary Mr D. Davenport
51 Hothersall Close
Coppenhall
Crewe

Cuerden Valley Park Lake, Elspeth
Mr R. Sharland
Lancashire Wild Life Trust
Shady Lane
Bamber Bridge, Preston
Telephone (01772) 324129
This venue has parking close to the water, but a key is needed from the Ranger to get onto the road that leads down to the water. This is an area of biological importance so care must be taken when moving or travelling to pegs.

Davenham Angling Club
The Secretary Mr A. Cook
RAFA Wings Club
Davenham, Cheshire
Davenham AC stock part of the River Dane with Trout, and this stretch is fly, spinner or worm only. There are concessionary rates for permits to disabled anglers on proof of disability.

Disabled Angling Federation, North West
The Hon/Sec Mr P. Sinnott
30 Brankstone Drive
Morecambe, LA4 5UL
This federation is a registered charity, and is only for wheelchair anglers.

Eller Beck Fisheries
Mrs Lawson
Eller Beck Farm
Brigham
Cockermouth
Telephone (01900) 825268
There are car parking and toilet facilities, and food is available on request.

Elworth Anglers
(Affiliated member of Cheshire AA)
The Secretary Mr P. Bradburn
62 Marriot Road
Elworth
Sandbach

Farnworth Centre NAA
The Secretary Mr A. Johnson
140 Buckley Lane
Farnworth, Bolton

Fir Tree Angling Society
The Secretary Mr R. Newport
8 Tunnicliffe New Row
Leigh, WN7 4TW
The society provides a concessionary permit to disabled anglers on proof of disability, and a concessionary permit for senior citizens. There are purpose built disabled pegs on Fir Tree Flash.

First Organisation First Rivington Ltd.
St Thomas Centre
Ardwick Green North
Manchester, M12 6S
Also, First Rivington Ltd
Mr Mike Hart
New Road
Anderton
Chorley, PR6 9HG
There is access for the disabled on all the waters, but prior arrangment should be made for Roddlesworth Reservoir (upper).

Frodsham District Angling Club
The Chairman Mr L. Heeson
C/o Frodsham Community Centre
Frodsham, Cheshire

Furness Fishing Association (Coarse Section)
The Secretary Mr P. Tickle
169 Blake Street
Barrow-in-Furness
Cumbria, LA14 5RS
All correspondence to:
Mr G. Grainger
44 Whinlatter Drive
Barrow-in-Furness

Furness Fishing Association (Game fishing section)

The Secretary Mr H. Atkinson
20 Sharp Street
Askam-in-Furness
Cumbria, LA16 7BN
Application for membership must be posted to the Secretary, full membership is only open to the residents living in the Furness area. Day tickets are issued at all local tackle shops, the season for tickets is from the 1st June until the last day of September.

Garswood Angling Society

The Secretary Mr B.G. Brown
28 Skelton Street
Bryn
Wigan, WN4 ODQ
Parking is within 10-20 yards of the society waters. All waters are well stocked and well looked after.

Gradus Angling Club

(Affiliated member of Cheshire AA)
The Secretary Mr D. Moore
7 Colwyn Crescent
South Reddish
Stockport

GEC Switchgear

(Affiliated member of Cheshire AA)
The Secretary Mr G. Brown
13 Heather Avenue
Droylsden
Manchester

Haslam Park Lake

Mr Crawled
Preston Borough Council
Leisure Services Department
Preston
There is parking close to the water, and approaches are accessible for wheelchairs. Concessionary permits are available on proof of disability.

Holly Bush Angling Club

(Affiliated member of Cheshire AA)
The Secretary Mr A. Culshaw
55 Hind Road
Wheelock
Sandbach
Cheshire

Hyndburn and Blackburn Angling Association

The Secretary Mr R. Clarke
14 Whipp Avenue
Clitheroe
This association has two waters with priority pegs for the disabled, ease of parking, and gives concessionary rates for disabled anglers.

Ingleborough Estate

Mr D.B. Holland
Ingleborough Estate
Clapham
Lancaster, LA2 8DR
Permits are weekly or season.

Ingleton Angling Association

The Secretary Mr N.W. Capstick
Bower Cottage
Uppergate
Ingleton, Nr Carnforth
Annual permit, day and weekly permits.

Keswick Angling Association

The Secretary Mr W. Ashcroft
Springhaven
How Lane
Portinscale
Keswick, CA12 5RS
Disabled anglers should get in contact with the Secretary of the association prior to fishing.

Kidsgrove and District Angling Association

The Secretary Mrs B. Rigby
95 Ian Road
Newchapel
Stoke-on-Trent
This association gives concessionary rates on proof of disability. Due to overhead power lines the Farm Pool is closed for fishing and is used as a stock pool; it will be opened as a fishery in the future.

King William IV, Newton Angling Society

The Secretary Mr S. Williams
51 Fairfield Road
Langley
Middleton,
Manchester, M24 4FZ
The Bottom Water has access for the disabled angler, with no parking restrictions. For further details contact the Secretary.

Kirkby Lonsdale Angling Association

G. Clough
Keepers Cottage
Burrow
Via Carnforth
Lancashire

Lancaster Centre NAA

The Secretary Mr K. Robinson
23 Goodwood Road
Lancaster

Lancashire County Council

Countryside Officer
County Planning Department
East Cliff County Offices
P.O. Box 160
Preston, PRl 3EX
Catch returns to be posted
There are public toilets, and refreshments on summer weekends.

Lancashire Fly Fishing Association

The Secretary Mr J. Winnard
Manor House
Grunsagill
Tosside
Nr Skipton
North Yorkshire, BD23 4SJ
Day tickets available for Dean Clough Reservoir, Gt Harwood, from Hyndburn Angling and Darts Centre, Accrington

Leigh and District Association of Anglers

The Secretary Mr T. Kelly,
70 Diamond Street,
Leigh
The association provides a concessionary permit to disabled anglers on proof of disability, and also to senior citizens. The association is willing to provide assistance if needed with prior notice to the Secretary.

Leyland Centre NAA

The Secretary Mr J. Pharaoh
3 West Paddock
Leyland, PR5 lHR
There are five local clubs within this centre. For information please contact the Secretary.

Liverpool and District Anglers Association

The Secretary Mr J. Johnson
97 Liverpool Road (North)
Maghull
Merseyside, L31 2HG
There are 8 clubs affiliated to this association. For details contact the Secretary of the association.

Longdendale Fly Fishing Association

The Secretary Mr A. Holmes
17 Crossmoor Crescent
Romiley
Stockport, SK6 4AG
There is parking within easy reach of the association's waters. Although the banking is not suitable for non-ambulant anglers, there is room for two wheelchairs on the pier.

Longton Pond Fishery

Mr C. Bowman
Crosshill Cottage
Blackford
Carlisle, CA6 4DU

Longton and District Angling Society

The Secretary Mr Stephen Butler
242 Stocks Road
Ashton
Preston
There are well constructed paths close to the banking, although the Ranger will have to be contacted to open access gates for cars or motorised chairs. Disabled pegs are to be constructed in the near future.

Lymm Angling Club

The Secretary Mr S. Griffiths
18 Manor Road
Lymm
Cheshire, WA13 OAY
The club is very progressive as can be seen by the species of fish that are stocked in some of their waters. Barbless hooks are compulsory on most waters, but are recommended to be used on all waters. No keepnets are allowed except in authorised matches. There are a number of waters that can be booked for matches, for details contact the Secretary.

Macclesfield and District Angling Association

(Affiliated member of Cheshire AA)
The Secretary Mr D. Ainsworth
3 Crowns
Rainbow Road
Macclesfield

Macclesfield Victoria

(Affiliated member of Cheshire AA)
The Secretary Mr C. Illingworth
23 Brookfield Lane
Macclesfield

Macclesfield Waltonians Angling Society

The Secretary Mr E. Bowyer
7 Ullswater
Macclesfield
Cheshire
There is very little access for non-ambulant disabled anglers due to high banking, although the society does have a number of disabled anglers as members.

Manchester Anglers Association

The Secretary Mr F. Fletcher
7 Alderbank Close
Kearsley
Bolton
Lancs, BL4 8JQ
All waters within this association are fly fishing only.

Manchester Recreational Services Department

The Director
Alexandra Centre Offices
2 Southcombe Walk
Moss Side
Manchester, M15 5NW
Parking is adjacent to Alexandra Park Lake, and permits for the disabled are concessionary on proof of disability. Assistance can be provided by prior arrangement.

Manchester and Salford Centre NAA

The Secretary Mr A. Morris
37 Tetlow Lane, Salford

Marsden Star Angling Society

The Sec Mr D. Brown
36 Western Avenue
Riddlesden
Keighley
West Yorkshire, BD20 5DJ
Annual permit and day ticket, there are no day tickets for the ponds, as they are strictly members only. The society gives concessionary rates to the disabled on proof of disability.

Mersey Valley Countryside Warden Service

The Water Park Manager Mr D. Barlow
Chorlton Water Park
Maitland Avenue
Chorlton-cum-Hardy
Manchester
Telephone (061) 491 1647
This water has good disabled access, and the service is in the process of establishing better paths with graded slopes, there are wheelchair platforms and restricted off road parking. A key is needed to gain access for registered disabled only, and can be obtained from the Park Warden. It must be stressed that this park is a site of biological importance with reference to wild life. There is a permanent warden presence around the park, and information can be sought from either the wardens or telephone (0161) 881 5639.

Mersey Centre NAA

The Secretary Mr R. Boardman
83 Beech Gardens
Rainford
St Helens
There are six clubs within this centre.

Middleport W.M.C.

(Affiliated member of Cheshire AA)
The Secretary Mr I. Davies
9 Heyburn Crescent
Dale Hall Burslem
Stoke-on-Trent

Mitre Angling Club

The Sec Mr R.D. Halstead
32 Parrock Road
Barrowford
Nelson
Lancashire, BB9 6QF

Mohmar Angling Club

(Affiliated member of Cheshire AA)
The Secretary Mr T. Kelly
61 Elm Drive
Crewe

Mow Cop Angling Club

(Affiliated member of Cheshire AA)
The Secretary Mr P. Carr
44 Victoria Avenue
Kidsgrove

Nantwich Angling Society

Mr J. Davies
28 Brown Avenue
Nantwich, CW5 7DH
The River Weaver in Nantwich is under joint control with Wych Anglers and has good access from public car parks.

National Rivers Authority, North West Region

Richard Fairclough House
P.O. Box 12
Knutsford Road
Warrington, WA4 lHG

National Rivers Authority Waters

River Lune
Halton and Skerton
Mr Shallis
Halton Stores
St Wilfreds Park
Halton, LA2 6PN
Mrs Curwen
Greenup Cottage
Hornby Road,Caton

River Ribble
Mitton Bridge to Calderfoot.
Mrs M. Haynes,
Mitton Hall Farm,
Mitton, Nr Whalley
All these waters are day ticket waters and the close season is enforced from the 15 March to 15 June.

National Trust, North West Region

The Hollens
Grasmere
Ambleside
Cumbria, LA22 9QZ
The National Trust is renown for its places of historic interest or natural beauty. They have a number of information centres that will give information on fishing waters that are accessible to the angler. Boating is allowed on its waters, canoes, rowing boats and sailing boats, but no powered craft are allowed on National Trust waters. Fishing from boats is by permit only. Launching is from areas open to the public. On some waters boats are available for hire from the National Trust. The use of lead weights for fishing is banned on all National Trust waters.

Nelson Disabled Anglers Association

The Secretary Mr L. Moorhouse
25 Moorhey Road
Little Hulton
Worsley, Manchester
This association is for disabled anglers only, both ambulant and non-ambulant.

Newton-le-Willows Anglers Association

The Secretary Mr G. Grice
10 Crown Street
Newton-le-Willows
Merseyside, WA12 9NP
There are parking facilities on both the top length and bottom length of the St Helens/ Sankey Canal at Newton-le-Willows.

Nor West Disabled Anglers Association

The Hon/Sec Mr N. Sedgewick
13 Alston Road
Welly
Wigan, WN2 lAU
This association is for disabled anglers only, both ambulant and non-ambulant. It has a water of its own, Widows Flash, where there are facilities for the disabled angler. It is open for day ticket to general anglers, but season permits are for disabled anglers only.

North Liverpool Anglers (Match Group)

The Secretary Mr J. Browne
33 Eleanor Road Bootle
Liverpool, L20 6BP
This match group has disabled anglers within the group.

Northern Anglers Association

The Hon/Sec Mr A.G.R. Brown
10 Dale Road
Golborne
Warrington
This association comprises approximately 150 affiliated clubs, which are within an area centre; the addresses for these centres are in alphabetical order within this section. If any angler wishes to avail themselves of any club or water within the centre area, they should use the addresses given to contact the Secretary of the centres enclosing an S.A.E. All affiliated clubs retain the rights to their own waters and the Northern Anglers' waters.

Northwich Anglers Association

The Hon/Sec Mr J. Glithero
P.O. Box 18
Northwich
Cheshire, CW9 5SE
This association has purchased a number of its own waters and woodlands which it preserves to safeguard the future for anglers and the general public. Most of the waters have parking facilities close to the fishing areas.
Disabled permits are complimentary to those receiving mobility allowance. Senior citizens must have been a member of the association for one year prior to applying for complimentary membership. Billinge Green has a purpose built wheelchair platform and an access road and ramp to lend assistance. All enquiries to be addressed to the Hon/Sec.

Orrell Angling Club

The Secretary Mr D. Bushell
62 Melwood Drive
Liverpool, L12 8NW

Padiham and District Angling Society

J.W. Whittam
58 Lingmoor Road
Burnley, BB12 8UY

Pendle Borough Council

Outdoor Recreation Manager
Bank House
Albert Road
Colne
Lancashire, BB8 OBP
The Council has three waters within its control, with varying access for disabled anglers, although only Bull Grove Lodge has fishing platforms which are able to take wheelchairs; for further information contact the Outdoor Recreation Manager.
One rod to be used at one time, not more than 2 hooks. Fishing hours: sunrise to dusk only.

Penrith Angling Association

Hon/Sec Mr A. Welling
Beck Bank Farm
Great Salkeld
Penrith
Cumbria, CAll 9NA
Most of the association waters are rivers, which have very little access for the disabled angler. Disabled are welcome, however, and the association gives concessionary rates on proof of disability.
Permits can be obtained from
C.R. Sykes, Tackle Shop
Great Dockray, Penrith
They are closed on Wednesdays, Sundays and Public Holidays.

Preston Centre NAA

The Secretary Mr R. Mayor
27 Shirley Lane
Longton
Preston, PR4 5WJ

Prestwich and Whitefield Angling Club

The Chairman Mr P. Davis
143 Clifton Road
Prestwich
Manchester, M25 7HG
There is no close season for full members of the club, but no keepnets are allowed between March 15th and June 15th inclusive. The club give concessionary rates to the disabled on proof of disability, and to senior citizens.

Radway Green Angling Society

(Affiliated member of Cheshire AA)
Mr W. Goodwin
50 Moorehouse Avenue
Alsager
Stoke-on-Trent

Ramsbottom Angling Association

The Secretary Mr A.F. Metca!fe
23 Westcombe Drive
Brandlesholme
Bury
Lancashire, BL8 lDN
Two of the waters are day ticket waters, the rest are on an annual permit basis whereby the annual permit holder may take a guest.
The majority of the waters have ease of access, and two of the waters it is possible to drive up to the waterside. This association has an ever increasing number of disabled members.

Redwell Fisheries

Arkholme
Over Kellett
Carnforth
Lancaster, LA6 lBQ
This fishery has ample parking, and large parties are welcome but prior booking is essential. Tackle is available for hire and trout are available for order.

Rochdale Metropolitan Borough Council

The Senior Warden
Visitors Centre
Rakewood Road
Littleborough, OL15 OAQ
Match bookings are available on this water.

Sale Centre NAA

The Secretary Mr K.S. Tolliday
13 Waverley Road
Sale

Salford Angling Club, Disabled Section

The Chairman Mr P. Yardley
4 Vicker Close
Swinton
Manchester, M27 2QD
This Disabled Section gives concessionary permits for disabled anglers on proof of disability, they are as follows:
Annual permit which allows disabled anglers to fish from Monday to Friday.
Full permit that allows all week round fishing.
A key is needed to enter this venue. For further details contact the Chairman.

Salford Inter Clubs Angling Association

The Secretary Mr A. Morriss
37 Tetlow Lane
Higher Broughton
Salford, M7 OBU
There are a number of fishing platforms for disabled anglers, but all cars must use the official car park, which is situated 1/4 mile from the water. Parking at Clowes Park is on the public highway.
No Bloodworm or Bloodworm feed allowed.

South Manchester Angling Club

The Secretary Mr D. Crookall
12 Wincombe Street
Rusholme
Manchester, M14 7PJ
Restricted annual permit or membership.
There is limited access for non-ambulant anglers, as there are four wide steps from the road to the bankside.

Southport and District Angling Association

The Secretary Mr M. Bannister
31A Botanic Road
Southport
The association has waters in the Martin Mere area. The fisheries are day ticket as well as annual permit. For details of waters available contact the Secretary.

Staveley and District Angling Association

The Secretary Mr D. Andrews
17 Rawes Garth, Staveley
Kendal
Cumbria
Day and weekly permits are available from: Woofs Newsagents, Main Street, Staveley.
Season permits are available from: The Permit Secretary, 18 Rawes Garth, Staveley.

St Helens Angling Association

The Secretary Mr L. Bromilow
4 Bassenthwaite Avenue
Moss Bank
St Helens, WAll 7AB
This association has a number of waters that have parking facilities, Carr Mill and the St Helens canal. Carr Mill Dam is a match venue of some repute.

St Helens Ramblers Angling Society

The Secretary Mr A. Twiss
47 Exeter Street
St Helens
Parking is on the road at the side of Paddock Dam.

Stockport and District Anglers Federation

The Secretary Mr H. Ollerenshaw
133 Manchester Road
Hyde
Cheshire, SK14 2BZ

This federation is made up of 65 separate clubs with their own waters. For details of these clubs, please write to The Secretary of the Federation.

At Etherow Country Park there are pegs for disabled anglers and parking close to the water. There is a cafe, and toilet facilities within easy reach. If help is needed contact the Warden's Office.

Disabled clubs can contact the Secretary of the federation to fish matches free Monday to Friday. Individuals are welcome but the Secretary should be contacted first.

Stoke-on-Trent Angling Society

Mr S.F. Broadgate
5 Kingsfield Oval
Basford, ST4 6HN

This society has a number of waters that have ease of access for the disabled angler.

Guest permits are available but guests must be accompanied by a member of the society.

Tame Valley Countryside Warden Service

Mr John Courtman
Countryside Warden
Stamford House
Jowetts Walk
Tameside, OL7 OBB

This water is a day ticket water with ease of access for disabled anglers and adapted pegs for wheechairs. There are toilet facilities

No keepnets except on organised matches.

Tarporley Angling Club

The Secretary Mr Clay
58 Church Hill Drive
Tarporley, CW6 OBZ

There is a car/coach parking area within 60 yards of the club's water, and a hard standing area for disabled anglers to fish from.

Tatton Park

The Director
Tatton Park
Knutsford
Cheshire, WA16 6QN
Telephone (01565) 654822
or Fax (01565) 650179

This park is owned by the National Trust, and is managed on their behalf by the Cheshire County Council, Heritage and Recreation Service. The park has an abundance of wild life, both Red and Fallow deer mingle with sheep and cattle that roam the park, so please drive carefully. Tickets can be purchased from the entry gates.

Todmorden Angling Society

The Secretary Mr R. Barber
12 Grisedale Drive
Manor Park Farm
Burnley, BB12 8AR

There is parking and access for wheelchair anglers and the waters are open all year round. The society has very active senior and junior sections.

Tootal Angling Club

(Affiliated member of Cheshire AA)
The Secretary Mr E. Woolf
14 Dunkeld Road
Wythenshaw
Manchester

Trafford Leisure Services

Principal Leisure Services Manager
P.O. Box 14
Town Hall
Talbot Road
Stretford
Greater Manchester, M32 OYZ

Warrington Anglers Association

The Hon/Sec Mr F. Lythgoe
52 Parker Street
Warrington (Club Premises)
Cicely Mill Pool has a portion of the banking as a wild life preserve, and no keepnets are allowed on this water. Unless otherwise stated all waters are one bank fishing only, or as stated in the Warrington Anglers permit.
There is a car park situated at Pickerings Bridge, Thelwall, and a purpose built ramp for wheelchair access which leads onto the Bridgewater Canal.
The association stocks all their waters as needed throughout the year.

Warrington Borough Council

Mr N. White (Head Ranger)
Community Services Directorate
Warrington Borough Council
Warrington
There is only limited parking for Longbarn Pond.

Wigan Centre NAA

The Secretary Mr W. Gratton
66 Balcarres Road
Asphull
Wigan
All centre waters are situated in the Wigan and Chorley area.

Wigan SIDC

This club is for disabled anglers only, which gives concessionary rates on proof of disability and with the committee's agrement. For details contact the Secretary of Wigan Centre NAA.

Wigan Metropolitan Borough Council

The waters that are controlled by the Council are day ticket waters, and all permits are available from the Rangers on site.
No keepnets or ground bait can be used other than in swim feeders.

Windermere, Ambleside and District Angling Association

The Hon/Sec Mr J.R. Newton
Brackenthwaite House
Black Beck Wood
Storrs Park
Windermere
Cumbria, LA23 3LF
This association has a number of permits which are as follows:
Full membership, which is only available to permanent residents living within 10 miles of St Mary's Church, Ambleside.
Associate membership, available to anglers not eligible to full membership; there is a waiting list for this permit.
All trout waters are limited to two fish only, but catch and release is encouraged.
Grasmere: Under no circumstances should anyone fish from the island or outside the association boundarys.
The following are only available for single fisheries:
Ghyll Head permit. Dubbs permit. Ratherheath permit. Cleabarrow permit. Holehird Tarn permit. High Newton Reservoir permit.
Many of the local hotels offer guests free fishing on association waters; details from hotel receptions and Tourist Information Centres.
There are also, Day, 7 Day and Year permits for visitors, details from Information Centres and local tackle shops. For further details contact the Hon/Sec.

Winsford and District Anglers Association

The Secretary Mr J.S. Baily
22 Peover Avenue
Winsford, CW7 lLA
The marina section on the River Weaver has parking and toilet facilities.
The association gives concessionary rates to disabled anglers on proof of disability. The association is currently looking at a project to provide 40 pegs for the disabled, and parking on the River Weaver.

Withnell Angling Club

The Secretary Mr M.P. Winterson
13 Larch Drive
Brinscall
Chorley, PR6 3QM
Membership Secretary
P.O. Box 41
Chorley, PR6 8JZ
With reference to Rakes Brook and Roddlesworth, the limit for taking trout is two fish not less than 10 inches in size.

Woodfold Farm Fisheries

Mr John Cornthwaite
Woodfold Farm
Whitechapel
Goosnargh
Preston, PR3 2ES
Telephone (01995) 40347
This fishery has parking close to the waters for the disabled and Mr Cornthwaite will lend assistance if needed; the access is going to be improved to assist wheelchairs.
Boilies, Groundbait, Bloodworm are not allowed.
This water is bookable for matches.

Wybunbury Angling Association

(Affiliated member of Cheshire AA)
The Secretary Mr P. Harding
325 Newcastle Road
Shavington
Crewe

Wyche Anglers

(Affiliated member of Cheshire AA)
The Secretary Mr F. McGarry
Wyche Anglers
London Road
Nantwich

Wyreside Lakes, Forton

Mr Collinson
Jenkinsons Farm
St Michaels
This fishery has ample parking close to the water, it also has a cafe, a tackle shop and toilet facilities.

Helping the disabled angler

NATIONAL FEDERATION OF ANGLERS

On behalf of the National Federation of Anglers commitee for the Disabled, I would like to recommend this book.

I have seen many attempts to produce a guide for anglers, including ones particular to the disabled; none has succeeded to the extent of this one. All the information required to find suitable waters is here.

There are many 'freelance' anglers who do not wish to join a club and take advantage of day-ticket waters. There are those on holiday who may wish to go fishing and need guidance to select suitable waters.

The specific requirements of the disabled (good access, ease of parking and a safe spot to fish from) are not always understood by many able bodied persons, anglers or not. This book provides the information the disabled, as well as the able bodied, seek in an easily understood manner.

I must congratulate Lawrence Millington on his diligence and patience in obtaining and collating all the information found here. In persuading so many individuals and organisations to provide the information he has succeeded where many have failed.

The advantages of keeping the area covered limited, has enabled a much more thorough approach and consequently more help for the angler seeking somewhere to fish.

I am sure this book will not only indicate the places to fish but will encourage non-anglers to try the sport, particularly people with disabilities and thus increase the number of people who gain pleasure from this most satisfying of pastimes.

Alan Bates,
Chairman, NFA Committee for the Disabled

NATIONAL FEDERATION OF ANGLERS

The National Federation of Anglers is the governing body for coarse angling. It is listened to with respect by Government, Sports Council, Environmental Organisations and the National Rivers Authority.

The N.F.A. operates through clubs to the eight regions who each have two representatives on the National Executive Council. From these members committees are formed to deal with the various aspects, such as Fisheries and Environmental Protection, Finance and Administration, Disabled, etc.

Annual conferences, where all clubs can be represented, formulate the main policies and guides the N.E.C. for the following year. The conference elects a President and three vice Presidents. The disabled are looked after by a committee and a system of Regional Officers for the Disabled (RODS), one in each region. Their brief is to assist the disabled to fish by being able to match up the disabled with suitable waters and to advise on fishing tackle and methods. They are frequently called upon to advise clubs and other organisations in creating fishing suitable for the disabled.

They are responsible for organising a Qualifying Match for the National Championship for the Disabled, which is held annually and managed by the Committee for the Disabled. Medals are awarded in exactly the same way as for all other National Championships. A Calender of Disabled Events is kept at the Derby office and is available both to organisers, who may wish to include their event, and to anglers.

The Federation welcomes any person interested in coarse angling for disabled to contact their Regional Officer or to directly to Headquarters where every effort will be made to deal with requests, offers, and provide suitable advice.

Addresses

N.F.A. Halliday House,
Eggington Junction,
Derbyshire,
DE65 6GU
Telephone
(01283) 734735
Fax (01283) 734799

North West Regional Officer:
Mr P. Neal Esq.
16 Kingston Gardens,
Hyde,
Cheshire, SK14 2DB
Telephone
(0161) 368 3290

NORTH WEST WATER Ltd

Whilst conservation is a main commitment of North West Water, the development and management of compatible recreational facilities is also a major requirement. This is the responsibility of the Recreation and Conservation section. Much of the North West Water's land includes designated conservation areas, or areas of access for the public which are of importance. Through consultation procedures with interested parties, sites of both ecological and historical importance are avoided or treated with sensitivity.

North West Water will continue to work towards making the countryside and facilities accessible to disabled persons both ambulant and non-ambulant, with the aim of maximizing their opportunities to use those facilities as independently as is reasonably possible, whilst allowing full integration with able-bodied people.

The awareness of the needs of the disabled has so far translated into the design of visitor facilities, which include ramps, ease of access for wheelchairs, toilet facilities, and generally keeping any hazards down to a minimum.

Every September, a number of organisations hold a sports day for people with disabilities which takes place at Rivington; staff are provided by North West Water to assist the organisers in planning and managing the numerous events.

For details of the above
Telephone 'Contact' (01204) 696118

There are a large number of reservoirs and lakes owned by North West Water that can be fished by the disabled angler, both ambulant and non-ambulant. These are managed by area officers which are as follows:

Northern Area (Cumbria, North Lancashire)
Mr Peter Guy,
Recreation and Conservation Officer.
Telephone (01772) 822200

Central Area (Central and South Lancashire, Wigan and Merseyside)
Mr Phil Luff,
Recreation and Conservation Officer.
Telephone (01204) 696118

Southern Area (Greater Manchester (except Wigan) Cheshire)
Mr George Grime,
Recreation and Conservation Officer.
Telephone (01457) 869133

If anyone would like to discuss either the nature or provision of facilities generally, or to come forward with further ideas for assisting people with disabilities, could they contact:

Recreation and Conservation Manager
North West Water,
Chadwick House,
Warrington Road,
Risley,
Warrington, WA3 6AE
or Telephone (01925) 857000

The British Sports Association for the Disabled - B.S.A.D.

The B.S.A.D. is a charitable organisation and was founded in 1961by Sir Ludwig Guttmann to provide and develop sport and recreation for people with disabilities, both ambulant and non-ambulant.
The B.S.A.D. provides, develops and co-ordinates opportunities in sport and recreation and is recognised by the Government in this role.
In order to fulfil its objectives the B.S.A.D. works in partnership with the relevant agencies, which include The British Paralympic Association, The United Kingdom Sports Association for People with a Mental Handicap, The National Disability Sports Organization and the Governing Bodies of Sport and The Sports Council.
There are approximately 50,000 members, 550 clubs, schools and associations in the ten regions of England.

Grants from governing bodies such as the Sports Council and charitable trusts enable the B.S.A.D. to promote opportunities, from the beginner to the elite disabled sportsmen and sportswomen. There are a number of commercial sponsors, from major banking and commercial concerns to private donations, which give assistance towards sports facilities for some of the National Championships, etc.

The Head Office is :
Mary Glen Haig Suite,
Solecast House,
13/27 Brunswick Place,
London, Nl 6DX
Telephone (0171) 490 4919
Fax (0171) 490 4914

The Northwest Regional Office is:
Sportsnet, C/o Leisure Services,
The Wellsprings,
Civic Centre,
Bolton, BL1 lUS
Telephone Mr P. Vickerman (01257) 470439
or Mr G. Clarke (01270) 759680
Fax (01204) 365034

United Kingdom Sports Association for People with Mental Handicap - U.K.S.A.P.M.H.

Nowadays there are many chances for us to play sport or exercise at whatever level we choose. But for a million people in the United Kingdom with a mental handicap (which is often termed 'learning difficulties') that freedom and the choice to participate does not exist. Their enthusiasm to play, compete and enjoy frequently meets many barriers which discourages them from taking part, this stems from loneliness, not knowing what their capabilities are, a lack of confidence and the attitudes of other people.

The U.K.S.A.P.M.H. is a registered charity and by working in partnership with other organisations the association helps to create new chances for people with mental handicap to participate whatever their particular interest or ability.

The association helps to promote sport and recreation for people with mental handicap both at home and abroad, it also helps to create an awareness of their capabilities and needs within the sports world and to the general public. The association also runs training courses, seminars for volunteers, sports coaches and staff who provide sport and recreational activities, which are arranged by the association at both local and national level.

The national office provides information on equipment, activities and the media; information is gathered and circulated through regular newsletters to keep organisations and individuals up-to-date. People can help in two ways, either by offering a little of their time, knowledge or expertise, or by making a donation. If you would like further information or feel you could help with any aspect of our work please contact the national office.

U.K.S.A.P.M.H.
30 Philip Lane, London, N15 4JB
Telephone (0181) 885 1177 Fax (0181) 885 4560
Registered Charity No. 281451

MENCAP AND FRIENDS

The Mencap and Friends Society was founded in 1988 with the sole idea of organising fishing outings for people with learning difficulties. In so doing they have the help of a number of able-bodied anglers, as well as ambulant and non-ambulant disabled anglers, who give assistance in a number of ways, advice, encouragement, etc., and who sit with the anglers on a one to one basis whilst fishing.

The handicapped anglers are picked up by sitting car ambulance and, on reaching the venue they then fish for a short period of time before partaking in a barbecue. They finish the day by fishing a short match and a good day is had by all.

There are six outings a year, and a presentation party is organised for a date after the last outing.

The Society was founded by
Mr Duncan Greenhalgh,
Telephone (01204) 708329
and Mr J.P. Corless,
Telephone (0161) 790 8168

If any individual or Club/Association would like to lend assistance in anyway would they contact
The Secretary Mr George A. Hunter,
20 Primrose Avenue,
Farnworth,
Bolton, BL4 ODP
or Telephone (01204) 700792

BRITISH WATERWAYS FISHING ON HOLIDAY

Holidaymakers in the North West will find plenty of opportunity to fish on British Waterways Fisheries. However, care is needed to ensure that a National Rivers Authority Rod Licence and correct permits are obtained. A permit is required to fish anywhere on the canals or reservoirs, even when fishing from a boat. Permits are readily available for British Waterways directly managed fisheries as set out below:

Shropshire Union Canal
40 miles of canal from Audlem to Ellesmere Port, including the Middlewich Branch
Day/Monthly/Season permits available

Ashton Canal
3 miles of the Canal Between Droylsden and Manchester
Day/Monthly/Season permits available

Llangollen Canal
45 miles of canal between Hurleston and Llangollen
Monthly permits only available

Rudyard Reservoir
170 acre reservoir Nr Leek
Day permits only, from the patrolling Ranger or from ticket machine located at the dam

Although British Waterways own the vast majority of the fishing, 80% of the canals are leased to angling clubs who make their own arrangements for issuing permits. Permits can be obtained from the following addresses:

Regional Fisheries Manager (North West)
British Waterways,
Navigation Road,
Northwich,
Cheshire, CW8 lBH
Telephone (01606) 74321 or Fax (01606) 871471

The following boatyards:

Shropshire Union Canal
Dartline, Bunbury
Nantwich Canal Centre, Nantwich
Holiday Afloat, Market Drayton

Trent and Mersey Canal
Middlewich Narrowboats, Middlewich

Llangollen Canal
English County Cruisers, Wrenbury
Viking Afloat, Whitchurch
Black Prince, Whixall
Maestermyn Cruisers, Oswestry
Anglo Welsh, Trevor

Rudyard Lake
Mr M. Booth,
Rudyard Lake Ranger Service,
Information Centre,
Lake Road,
Rudyard, Nr Leek,
Staffordshire, ST13 8XB
Telephone (0153) 833 280

FACILITIES FOR DISABLED ANGLERS

Level banks and frequent access generally make British Waterways Canals suitable for the disabled. Some stretches have particularly easy access allowing anglers in wheelchairs to approach the water's edge. Most of the canal system is let to angling clubs and some of these offer special facilities for disabled anglers.

Many clubs issue day permits but, on some lengths, it may be necessary to join the club to fish a particular spot. Familiarity with the water will enable each angler to discover individual sites suited to his particular needs, but some of the most easily accessible venues on those fisheries directly managed by British Waterways are as follows:

Shropshire Union Canal
The ambulant disabled angler will find many urban locations close to parking and accessibility. It is possible to approach the waters edge in a wheelchair at several spots in Chester, Ellesmere Port and Audlem and some of these lengths are being specially stocked.

Ashton Canal
There are several places where it is possible to park very close to the canal and gain access to the bank. These include Fairfield and Ancoats Locks, the swing bridges (No. 14 & 15) near Fairfield. Stretches near locks are suitable during the winter months when boat traffic is low.

Rudyard Lake
The proximity of pegs to access points make parts of the lake, particularly the north-eastern bank, suitable for the ambulant disabled, though the fluctuating water levels mean that there is often a short climb or scramble to the water itself. A Ranger has been recently appointed and it is hoped that this approach to the pegs can be improved. Parking for the severely disabled person can usually be arranged close to the information centre by prior contact.

For more information contact Mr M. Booth,
Rudyard Lake Ranger Service,
Information Centre,
Lake Road,
Rudyard, Nr Leek,
Staffordshire, ST13 8XB
Telephone (0153) 833 280

The Waterways Code for Anglers

The Waterways Code for Anglers provides practical advice to help you, and others, to enjoy fishing British Waterways canals, rivers and reservoirs in safety.

Courtesy

Do not dig out banks, or remove pitching stones, or clear away vegetation. If you feel conditions should be improved, please contact your local Waterway Manager. Make sure you choose a site away from the outside of bends as this is where deep draughted craft need to travel. People aboard moored craft appreciate their privacy, so try and fish at least 50 feet away. A boater has priority at official mooring points, move your tackle in good time.

Please take your litter, food or bait home with you, or find a bin. Carelessly discarded bait may encourage vermin, and if thrown in the water may spoil the fishing for others. When a boat approaches, raise your line well in advance and keep it well clear of the passing craft and anyone aboard it.

Take care not to block the towpath with your fishing tackle. Look out for others when casting.

Safety

Check the towpath behind you when breaking down roach poles. Be careful when reaching out to retrieve lost tackle, or when playing particularly large fish. Always check for the presence of overhead power lines before starting to fish, and never fish within 100 feet of them.

Always comply with the warning signs, and do not walk along with your rod held upright.

Pollution presents extreme danger to wildlife and fish. Should you see any please contact your local Waterway Manager or dial 100 and ask for Freephone Canals. It is dangerous for children to fish near locks and sluices.

Health

The quality of water in our canals, rivers and reservoirs is generally good but, unlike tap water, it is untreated and micro-organisms are naturally present. The risk of contracting illness is small (including the much publicised, but extremely rare, Weil's disease).

You should take some sensible precautions such as covering any cuts before exposure to water, not swallowing the water, avoiding full immersion, washing with clean water after any contact, and don't put wet fishing line, rope or other objects in your mouth.

You should also be aware of blue-green algae which, although naturally present in many waters, under certain conditions produces a 'bloom' particularly along the edge of reservoirs after long periods of hot weather. The bloom forms a paint-like scum on the surface of the water and can be toxic to humans, dogs and livestock.

Avoid contact with the scum. Where it is known to be present, the NRA will issue a public notice and advise known user groups.

Should any accidental contact occur, wash from the skin as soon as possible. Should you become ill within two weeks of exposure to canal, river, or reservoir water, let your doctor know that you have been in contact with untreated water, especially if you have swallowed some.

Should you require local contact details or any further information about unpowered boating on our waterways and reservoirs, please contact:

Customer Services,
British Waterways,
Greycaine Road, Watford,
Hertfordshire, WD2 4JR
Telephone (01923) 226422

Fishery Byelaws

While every effort was made to ensure that these byelaws were correct at the time of going to press, byelaws are subject to periodic revision. Therefore, anglers are advised to acquire the latest copy of the byelaws for the North West region from:

NRA North West Region
Richard Fairclough House
Knutsford Road
Warrington, WA4 1HG

Anglers are also advised that each region of the NRA operates under a different set of byelaws.

1. Annual close season for fishing for salmon and trout (other than with rod and line)

The annual close season for fishing for salmon and trout (other than with rod and line) shall be the period from and including the 1st day of September to and including the 31st day of March following except in the Solway Firth where the annual close season shall be the period from and Including the 10th day of September to and including the 24th day of February following.

2. Annual close season for salmon (rod and line)

The annual close season for salmon (rod and line) shall be the period from and including the 1st day of November to and including the 31st day of January following with the following exception:
In the River Eden and all rivers, lakes and waters, tributary to or connected with the River Eden the period from and including the 15th day of October to and including the 14th day of January following.

3. Annual close season for migratory trout (rod and line)

The annual close season for fishing for migratory trout with rod and line shall be the period from and including the 16th day of October to and including the 30th day of April following except in the Rivers Annas, Bleng, Cumbrian Esk, Mite, Irt, Calder and Ehen and all rivers, lakes and waters tributary to or connected with those rivers where the annual close season shall be the period from and including the 1st day of November to and including the 30th day of April following.

4. Annual close season for non-migratory trout other than rainbow trout (rod and line)

The annual close season for fishing for non-migratory trout other than rainbow trout with rod and line shall be the period from and including the 1st day of October to and including the 14th day of March following.

5. Annual close season for rainbow trout (rod and line)

The annual close season for fishing for rainbow trout with rod and line shall be the period from and including the 1st day of October to and including the 14th day of March following except that in all lakes reservoirs and enclosed waters there shall be no statutory close season for rainbow trout.

Anglers must be in possession of a National Rivers Authority Rod Licence before fishing

6. Annual close season for char (rod and line)

The annual close season for fishing for char with rod and line shall be the period from and including the 1st day of October to and including the 14th day of March following except in the following waters where the annual close season shall be as stated:

(I) In Coniston Water, the period from and including the 1st day of November to and including the 30th day of April following.

(II) In Lake Windermere, the period from and including the 1st day of October to and Including the 30th day of April following, provided that it shall be lawful from and including the 15th day of March to fish for char with artificial lures from a moving boat.

7. Annual close season for freshwater fish

The annual close season for fishing for freshwater fish in rivers, streams and those parts of rivers canalised for navigation purposes shall be the statutory period, that is, the period from and including the 15th day of March to and including the 15th day of June following. On all other waters there shall be no statutory close season for freshwater fish.

8. Annual close season for eels

The annual close season for fishing for eels in non tidal parts of rivers, streams and those parts of rivers canalised for navigation purposes shall be the period from and including the 15th day of March to and including the 15th day of June following.

There shall be no close season for fishing for eels with rod and line in tidal waters.

There shall be no close season for fishing for eels with instruments other than rod and line in waters not frequented by salmon and trout.

It shall be lawful to fish for eels with a rod and line during the annual close season for rainbow trout.

9. The weekly close time for salmon and trout (other than with rod and line)

The weekly close time for fishing for salmon and trout (other than with rod and line) shall be the period between the hour of six on Saturday morning and the hour of six on the following Monday morning with the following exceptions:

(I) In the Solway Firth the period between the hour of six on Saturday morning andthe hour of twelve midnight on the following Sunday.

(II) In the Ellen Protected Area the period between the hour of six on Thursday morning and the hour of six on the following Monday morning.

10. Authorised fixed engines

For the purpose of Section 6 of the Salmon and Freshwater Fisheries Act 1975, the placing and use of fixed engines within the Authority's area (not being places within the sea fisheries district of a local Fisheries Committee) is hereby authorised in the following circumstances:

(I) Deleted

(II) When used by the owner of a fish farm or his agents or employees in the normal course of fish farming activity within the confines of that fish farm.

(III) Where the trap consists of a fixed trap, a moveable trap (which may be baited) or a fyke net licensed for the purpose of taking eels.

(IV) For taking sea fish provided that where the engine consists of a net or trap it is covered at all states of the tide by a minimum of 3 metres of water and is set seawards of the seawards boundary of the local Sea Fisheries Committee.

Don't use fishing poles or rods near overhead electric wires: it could be fatal!

11. Limitation of netting

The use of any net (not being an authorised fixed engine or a landing net used in conjunction with a rod and line) for taking salmon, trout, freshwater fish, or eels is prohibited except for the licensed use of the stated types of nets in the following parts of the Authority's area:

(a) In the Solway Firth - heave or haaf nets.

(b) In the Cumbrian Coastal Waters excluding the Ellen Protected Area, the Derwent Protected Area, the Ehen/Calder Protected Area and the Irt/Esk Protected Area as defined - drift, hang or whammel nets.

(c) In the Duddon Estuary - draw, draft or seine nets.

(d) In the Leven Estuary - lave nets.

(e) In the Kent Estuary - lave nets.

(f) (I) In the Lune Estuary - heave or haaf nets.

(II) In the Middle Lune Estuary - draw, draft or seine nets.

(III) In the Lower Lune Estuary - drift, hang or whammel nets.

(g) In the Ribble Estuary - drift, hang or whammel nets.

(h) In the Ellen Protected Area - heave or haaf nets.

(i) In the whole of the Authority's area:

(I) any net necessarily and solely used for the purpose of removing from an authorised fixed engine the fish caught by that fixed engine, or

(II) to any person using a net of any kind with the prior permission in writing of the Authority, and subject to any conditions contained therein, or

(III) The use of hand held dip nets for taking elvers.

Hooks and line are lethal to wildlife, so take them home

12. Regulation of nets

(I) Drift, hang or whammel nets shall for the purpose of these byelaws be unarmoured nets without bags or pockets, consisting of a single sheet of netting measuring when wet -

(a) When used in the Ribble Estuary, not more than 140 metres in length and not more than 34 meshes deep at any point and having meshes not less than 82mm in extension from knot to knot, or 328mm round the four sides;

(b) When used in the Lower Lune Estuary, not more than 300 metres in length and not more than 44 meshes deep at any point and having meshes not less than 63mm in extension from knot to knot or 252mm round the four sides;

(c) When used in any other part of the Authority's area not more than 300 metres in length and not more than 55 meshes deep at any point and having meshes not less than 50mm in extension from knot to knot or 200mm round the four sides.

(II) Heave or haaf nets shall, for the purposes of these byelaws be of single netting of a mesh measuring when wet not less than 50mm in extension from knot to knot, or 200mm round the four sides and shall be so constructed as to form a bag or purse suspended from a wooden frame, consisting of a heave, beam, or pole not exceeding 5.5 metres in length having at each end an end stick or projecting arm not exceeding 1.25 metres in length except that within the Solway Firth the mesh shall measure when wet not less than 44mm from knot to knot or 176mm round the four sides and the end sticks or projecting arms shall not exceed 1.9 metres.

(III) Lave nets shall, for the purposes of these byelaws be of single netting of a mesh measuring when wet not less than 50mm in extension from knot to knot or 200mm round the four sides and which shall be constructed to form a bag or purse attached to a yoke in the shape of a 'V', the widest part of which shall not exceed 2 metres, and which shall be fitted with a hand staff to the apex of the yoke.

(IV) Draw, draft or seine nets shall, for the purposes of these byelaws, be unarmoured nets without bags or pockets consisting of a single sheet or wall of netting, having meshes measuring when wet not less than 50mm in extension from knot to knot or 200mm round the four sides and a length of not more than 275 metres with the exceptions that when used in the Middle Lune and Duddon estuaries the nets shall have the following measurements when wet, namely: a length of not more than 185 metres and a depth on the middle of the net of not more than 144 meshes.

(V) The net and leader of a fyke net shall, together, not exceed 14 metres in length. The leader shall not exceed 10 metres in length and its height shall be no greater than the net aperture. Fyke nets and leaders shall be constructed of twine not less than Imm in diameter. Mesh size measured when wet shall not be less than 10mm in extension from knot to knot or 40mm round the four sides or more than 15mm from knot to knot or 60mm round the four sides. No net ring or hoop shall exceed 75cm in diameter. Wing nets shall not be used instead of a single leader.

(VI) Where moveable traps (which may be baited) are used for eel fishing no leader or wing nets shall be allowed. The dimensions of a moveable trap (which may be baited) shall not exceed 1.5m in length x 0.75m high x 0.75m wide if rectangular or 1.5m in length x 0.75m diameter if cylindrical. The trap if constructed of mesh shall have a mesh size measured when wet not less than l0mm in extension from knot to knot or 40mm round the four sides or more than 15mm from knot to knot or 60mm round the four sides.

(VII) An otter guard shall be fitted to the aperture of every fyke net or eel trap. This guard shall consist of either taut material with a mesh size measured when wet not more than 75mm from knot to knot or 300mm round the four sides, or a rigid grill with bars separated by not more than 85mm, or a ring guard with a diameter not more than 95mm.

(VIII) Dip nets for taking elvers shall not exceed 75cm in width or 1 metre in length exclusive of any handle.

(IX) For the purposes of paragraphs (I), (II),(III), (IV), (V), (VI) and (VII) of this byelaw measurements from knot to knot shall be in relation to each side of the square of the mesh;

(X) The use of any net made wholly or partly of mono-filament material for taking salmon, trout, freshwater fish or eels is prohibited.

13. Regulation of use of nets

Where, under the provisions of byelaw 11 the use of any of the nets therein mentioned is permitted, such nets shall not be used in any manner except that prescribed by the succeeding paragraphs of this byelaw.

(I) The manner of using a drift, hang or whammel net shall be as follows, namely it shall be shot or paid out from a boat and the boat and net attached shall float or drift freely with the tide. No drift, hang or whammel net or any part there of, shall be used within 185 metres from any part of another drift, hang or whammel net already in use;

No drift, hang or whammel net shall be worked across more than three quarters of the water in the channel at the time of fishing;

(II) The manner of using a heave or haaf net shall be by one person supporting or holding the net and lifting or scooping any fish that may become enclosed in the net;

(III) The manner of using a lave net shall be by one person standing or moving in the water and supporting or holding the net and lifting or scooping any fish. No person shall use a lave net in proximity to a fixed net, designed to catch other fish, in such a way that the migratory fish are restricted in movement by such fixed net thereby facilitating their taking in the lave net;

(iv) The manner of using a draw, draft or sein net shall be as follows, namely one end of the rope of the net shall be held on the shore or bank and the net shall be shot out or paid out from a boat which shall start from such shore or bank, and return thereto without pause or delay, and the net shall thereupon be drawn into and landed on such shore or bank and no net shall be shot out or paid out from any point within 90 metres from any part of the space on the shore or bank between the point of starting and the point of return of the boat during the said operation or until after expiration of 15 minutes from the time at which the net is complety drawn in and landed. No draw, draft or seine net shall be worked across more than three-quarters of the water in the channel at the time of fishing.

The hand ropes attached to the ends of the net shall not be considered part of such net.

(v) A fyke net and leader shall be fished parallel with the flow in the watercourse and without the previous permission of the Authority nets may only be set individually or in pairs and no part of any net or pair of nets shall be set closer than 30 metres to any part of any other net or pair of nets.

14. Numbering of licences, nets and boats

Any number bearing label issued by the Authority in respect of a licensed net shall at all times while the net is being used for fishing be attached to the headrope of the net or, in the case of a heave or haaf net, to that part most nearly corresponding to the headrope. Except that in the case of heave or haaf nets it shall not be an offence if the label is carried on the person of the licence holder when operating the net.

Every fyke net or moveable eel trap (which may be baited) shall be marked with the identity label bearing the number of the licence issued by the Authority which shall be fixed to the top of the front ring or hoop at the function with the leader. Any marker buoy attached to the net or trap shall clearly display the number of the licence relating thereto issued by the Authority.

The same number shall be conspicuously painted and maintained in white numerals not less than 150mm high and 20mm wide, on a black background or in black numerals on a white background, on the outside and near the centre of the gunwale on each side of the boat from or in connection with which the net is used. Provided that this byelaw shall not apply to boats that are already displaying numbers as required by the Merchant Shipping (Fishing Boats Registry) Order 1927 (S.I. 1927/ 642).

15. Carrying of nets during annual close season

No person shall, during the annual close season for salmon, carry or permit to be carried in any boat any net capable of taking salmon, other than a landing net or a net commonly used in the area for sea fishing if carried in a boat or vessel commonly used for that purpose.

16. Carrying of unlicensed nets

The carrying in or attaching to a boat or vessel whilst being used in fishing for salmon or trout of any net (other than a landing net) which does not comply with the type or dimensions set out in byelaw 12 or if it does comply with that byelaw does not have the label described in byelaw 14 attached to it, is hereby prohibited.

17. Removal of fish

No person may take or remove from any waters within the area of the Authority without lawful authority any salmon, trout, freshwater fish or eels, whether alive or dead.

18. Baiting

During the period from and including the 15th day of March to and including the 15th day of June in any year in rivers, streams, those parts of rivers canalised for navigation purposes and in the following lakes:

Windermere, Coniston, Rydal Water, Grasmere, Ullswater, Brothers Water, Bassenthwaite, Derwentwater, Loweswater, Crummock Water, Buttermere, Ennerdale Water and Wastwater,

(I) fishing will only be allowed with minnow, worm, shrimp, prawn or artificial flies or lures; and

(II) the use of any lure or bait not on or attached to a hook is prohibited.

Leave your peg tidy, do not leave food it encourages vermin

19. Prohibition of taking undersized fish

No person shall take from any waters within the area any fish of a kind and of a size less than such size as is hereinafter prescribed, that is to say:

Migratory trout	300mm
Brown trout and char	200mm
Chub and barbel	250mm
Grayling, tench, bream and carp	230mm
Roach, perch, rudd, crucian carp and dace	200mm
Gudgeon and ruffe	100mm

The size shall be ascertained by measuring from the tip of the snout to the fork or cleft of the tail.

Provided that this byelaw shall not apply to any person who:

(I) Takes any undersized fish unintentionally if he at once returns to and liberates the same in the water with as little injury as possible.

(II) Takes any undersized fish, other than salmon or trout, keeps the same alive in a keep net and then, on the same day as he took them, returns such fish to, and liberates them in, the same water from which he took them.

(III) Takes any undersized fish other than salmon or trout and uses them as bait on the same day and on the same water from which he took them provided that at any one time he does not have in his possession more than ten such fish alive or dead.

(IV) Being the owner or occupier of a fish farm (or the servant or the agent of any such owner or occupier) takes any undersized fish from that fish farm.

20. Keep nets

(I) On rivers, streams, those parts of rivers canalised for navigation purposes and in the following lakes, no person shall use a keep net or any other means of retaining any kind of fish during the statutory close season for coarse fish:

Windermere, Coniston, Rydal Water, Grasmere, Ullswater, Brothers Water, Bassenthwaite, Derwentwater, Loweswater, Crummock Water, Buttermere, Ennerdale Water and Wastwater.

(II) No person shall use a keep net:

(a) Of less than 2.0 metres in extended length;

(b) With rings less than 380mm in diameter or if rectangular less than 355mm by 255mm;

(c) With wider spacing of rings than one ring per 300mm excluding the top ring;

(d) With a mesh size of more than 16mm measured diagonally from knot to knot when stretched and wet.

(III) The use of keep nets commonly known as micromesh nets is permitted. In the case of such nets the width of the mesh measured when wet but unstretched shall not exceed 8mm and such nets shall comply with (II)(a), (b) and (c) above.

21. Gaffs

The use of a gaff is prohibited at all times.

22. Fishing near weirs

No person shall, without the previous consent in writing of the Authority, during the period between the 30th day of September and the first day of the salmon close season for rod and line in any year, take or attempt to take by any means, any fish within a distance of 20 metres above and 50 metres below the crest of any man-made construction which impounds water in the rivers and streams of the River Ribble catchment upstream of the Naze at Freckleton (excluding the River Darwen, River Calder and the River Douglas), and in all rivers and streams north of the Ribble catchment.

In respect of the undermentioned weirs no person shall at any time take or attempt to take by any means, any fish within a distance of 20 metres above and 50 metres below the crest of the said weirs:

Branthwaite Weir	River Marron
Calder Hall Pumphouse Weir	River Calder (W. Cumbria)
Stramongate Weir	River Kent
Holmehead Weir	River Caldew
Cummersdale Weir	River Caldew
Buckabank Weir	River Caldew

and in respect of the undermentioned weir no person shall at any time take or attempt to take by any means, any fish within a distance of 20 metres above and 75 metres below the crest of the said weir.

Ennerdale Mill Weir	River Ehen

No persons shall at any time without the prior consent of the Authority in writing, take or attempt to take by any means any fish within a fish pass or within a 5 metres radius of either the entrance to or exit from any fish pass.

23. Worm fishing

No person shall, excepting as hereinafter provided, use in fishing for salmon or trout a worm baited on more than a single hook and such hook shall not exceed 40mm in length overall nor 15mm in width of gape and the weight or weights used to sink the hook shall not in any case exceed 30g in the aggregate; provided that a tackle of two or three hooks may be so used if tied one above the other upon a single strand of gut or other artificial substitute material and if each of such hooks does not exceed 15mm in length and is not more than 8mm in width of gape.

24. Size of hooks and weight of lures

(a) No person shall use in fishing with rod and line for salmon or trout after the 31st day of August in any year double, treble or multiple hooks any of which exceed 8mm gape provided that this shall not apply to a person fishing with an artificial fly not exceeding 15g in weight.

(b) No person shall use in fishing with rod and line for salmon or trout after the 31st day of August in any year any lure or weight which (together or singly) exceed 30g in weight.

The provisions of this byelaw shall not apply to the following listed rivers and all rivers lakes and waters tributary to or connected with those rivers:

Rivers Eden, Esk (Border), Derwent, Ellen, Waver, Wampool, Annas, Bleng, Esk, Mite, Irt, Calder and Ehen nor to fishing for char in lakes Windermere, Ennerdale, Coniston, Rydal Water and Grasmere.

25. Return of foul hooked fish

All salmon and migratory trout hooked otherwise than in the mouth shall be returned to the water as soon as practicably possible and with as little injury as possible.

26. Prohibition of fishing in certain waters in Kendal

The use for taking salmon, trout, freshwater fish or eels of any instrument in such part of the River Kent as lies between Victoria Bridge and its confluence with the former Dockray Hall mill race situated 400 metres upstream of Victoria Bridge in the Borough of Kendal by a person fishing from the right (westerly) bank of the said river at any time is prohibited.

This byelaw shall not apply to fly fishing with rod and line providing that no weight or weighted device is attached to or incorporated in the line, cast or hook.

27. Use of lead weights

(1) Subject to paragraph (2) below, no person shall use for taking salmon, trout, freshwater fish or eels in any waters within the Authority's Area any instrument to which is attached, directly or indirectly, any lead weight.

(2) Paragraph (1) above does not prohibit the use of a lead weight of 0.06 grams or less (No.8 shot), or of more than 28.35 grams (1oz).

28. Returns of net and rod catches

Any person to whom a licence is issued to fish for salmon or migratory trout within the Authority's area shall, on a form provided by the Authority;

(a) In the case of netsmen, send to the Authority on the last day of the months of March, April, May, June, July, August and September a return showing each date fished and the number of tides fished on that date, the individual weight of each fish taken and the river and location where caught. If no fish are taken during a day's fishing, the return should indicate that no fish were taken on that day.

(b) In the case of anglers, send to the Authority in the month of November a return showing the individual weight of each fish taken and the date, river and location where caught, together with a statement of the number of days spent on each river fished including days where no fish were caught.

Anglers are requested to observe the Country Code

29. Returns of net catches for eels

Any person fishing for eels otherwise than with rod and line in the Authority's area shall in the month of January in each year either:

(1) Send a return to the Authority in the appropriate form provided by the Authority giving particulars of any eels he has taken within the Authority's area during the period specified, or

(2) If he has taken no eels send to the Authority a Statement that he has taken no eels during such period.

30. Application

Except for byelaw 10 (authorised fixed engines), these byelaws shall not apply to any employee of the Authority acting in his official capacity or to any person who with the permission in writing of the Authority and acting in accordance with any conditions attached to that permission carries out work connected with the maintenance improvement and development of a fishery or for some scientific purpose.

31. Revocation of existing byelaws

All presently subsisting byelaws made by the Authority under powers conferred by Section 28(6) and Schedule 3 of the Salmon and Freshwater Fisheries Act 1975 shall be deemed to be revoked as and when each such byelaw is superseded by a new relevant or corresponding byelaw and when the said new byelaw is duly confirmed by the Minister.

Anglers must be in possession of a National Rivers Authority Rod Licence before fishing

32. Interpretation

(i) In these byelaws unless the context otherwise requires "Authority" means the National Rivers Authority.

"Authority's Area" means the area of the Authority as defined in Section 2(2) of and in Schedule 1 and paragraph 4 of Schedule 2 to the Water Act 1973.

"River Lune Byelaws" means byelaws made by the Authority regulating the Annual Close Season for salmon (rod and line) in the River Lune and theWeekly Close Time for salmon and trout (other than rod and line) in the estuary of the River Lune and confirmed by the Minister of Agriculture Fisheries and Food on 6th July 1983.

"Skerton Weir Byelaws" means byelaws made by the Authority regulating fishing at Skerton Weir on the River Lune and confirmed by the Minister of Agriculture, Fisheries and Food on 15th February 1979.

"Solway Firth" for the purposes of these byelaws means those tidal waters and parts of the sea within the Authority's area between a line drawn from the centre of the Golf Hotel at Powfoot at national grid reference NY14686546 to the eastern extremity of Grune Point at national grid reference NY14395684 and:

(i) In the River Esk (Border) a line drawn across the river from national grid referenceNY32456503 to national grid reference NY32456632.

(ii) In the River Eden a line drawn across the river from national grid reference NY33656182 to national grid reference NY33656155.

"Year" means the period from and including 1st January to and including 31st December following.

(II) For the purposes of byelaws 11, 12 and 13:

"Cumbrian Coastal Waters" means those tidal waters and parts of the sea to a distance of six nautical miles measured from the baselines from which the breadth of the territorial sea is measured adjoining the coast of Cumbria between the western limit of the Solway Firth and a line running true south-west from the summit of Black Combe at national grid reference SD135855.

"Ellen Protected Area" means those tidal waters and parts of the sea within a radius of 3 kms (1.6188 nautical miles) from the beacon at the seaward end of the south pier at Maryport.

"Derwent Protected Area" means those tidal waters and parts of the sea within a radius of 3 kms (1.6188 nautical miles) from the beacon on the south pier at Workington.

"Ehen/Calder Protected Area" means those tidal waters and parts of the sea within a radius of 3 kms (1.6188 nautical miles) from the centre of the railway bridge over the River Calder at national grid reference NY025027.

"Irt/Esk Protected Area" means those tidal waters and pans of the sea within a radius of 4 kms (2.1584 nautical miles) from the railway station at Ravenglass.

"Duddon Estuary" means that part of the estuary of the River Duddon seaward of a line drawn through Dunnerholme Point and Green Road Railway Station.

"Leven Estuary" means that part of the estuary of the River Leven seaward of a line drawn parallel to and 350m below the Leven Viaduct near Ulverston.

"Kent Estuary" means that part of the estuary of the River Kent seaward of a line drawn parallel to and 350m below the Kent Viaduct at Arnside.

"Lune Estuary" means that part of the estuary of the River Lune seaward of Carlisle Bridge in the City of Lancaster.

"Middle Lune Estuary" means that part of the estuary of the River Lune which lies seaward of a line drawn true south-east from the landward end of the breakwater at Bazil Point.

"Lower Lune Estuary" means that part of the estuary of the River Lune which lies seaward of a line drawn from Cockersand Abbey lighthouse to the seaward extremity, at high water springs, of Sunderland Point.

"Ribble Estuary" means that part of the estuary of the River Ribble which lies seaward of a line drawn due south from the Naze at Freckleton.

Always check that you have the correct permit before fishing, and if disabled that there is adequate access

(III) for the purpose of Byelaw 5:

"enclosed waters" means waters from which or into which fish cannot normally swim to or from the other waters.

(IV) For the purposes of Byelaw 27:

"Lead" includes any alloy or compound lead;

"Lead weight" means split shot or any other thing suitable for weighting fish lines which is neither incorporated and fully enclosed in the core of a fishing line nor incorporated in the construction of a swim-feeder, a self cocking float or a fishing lure.

(V) For the purposes of Byelaw 10,

"fixed engine" shall have the same meaning as in the Salmon and Freshwater Fisheries Act 1975.

Note: Byelaws 1-29, 31 and 32 were confirmed by the Minister on 11th October 1989. Until Byelaw 30 is confirmed, the old Byelaw 26 (which was confirmed by the Minister on 29th February, 1984, and which is reproduced below) will continue in force.

26. Application

These byelaws shall not apply to any employee of the Authority acting in his official capacity or to any person who with the permission in writing of the Authority and acting in accordance with any conditions attached to that permission carries out work connected with the maintenance improvement and development of a fishery or for some scientific purpose.

Pollution incidents should be reported to the nearest NRA area office, viz:

Carlisle	01228 25151
Bamber Bridge, Preston	01772 39882
Sale	0161 973 2237

NRA WELCOMES MINISTERS' RESPONSE ON CLOSE SEASON

The National Rivers Authority has accepted, in principle, ministerial modifications to byelaws proposed by the NRA for the coarse fish close season in England and Wales. Mr Michael Jack, Minister of State at the Ministry of Agriculture, Fisheries and Food (MAFF), has said that ministers intend to accept the NRA's proposal for a statutory close season on all rivers, streams and drains. They did not support the proposed extension of the statutory close season to all canals in England and Wales. Most importantly, ministers have indicated that they are prepared to accept, in general, the NRA's proposal that a close season on still waters should be at the discretion of fisheries owners. However, where the conservation of Sites of Special Scientific Interest (SSSIs) might be affected by a change, ministers have suggested that the close season should be retained. English Nature and the Countryside Council for Wales are currently preparing a list of SSSIs concerned.

David Jordan, NRA Head of Fisheries said: "The NRA believes that its original proposals provided the most logical and consistent solution to the existing hotch-potch of close season regulations. Nevertheless, the ministers' decision will provide a significant improvement over the current arrangements and, for this reason, we welcome their decision and will take forward the changes for the coming season. The continued inconsistency on canals is of concern to the NRA and we will be considering this matter further over the coming year."

The NRA submitted its proposals to MAFF for changes to the close season byelaws in December 1994 following extensive consultation with anglers, fishery owners, representative bodies for the sport and a wide range of other interests. Included in these changes was the proposal that all canal fisheries should, like rivers, be subject to a statutory close season. At present there is no statutory close season on canals in the South West or on most canals in the north of England. This situation remains unchanged at present as a result of the ministers' decision. The statutory close season for coarse fishing runs from 15 March to 15 June inclusive, but has been dispensed with in parts of England and Wales over the years. In the North West, canals and still waters are currently exempt from the coarse fish close season. The new ruling means that canals will remain exempt and the imposition of a close season on still waters will be at the discretion of the owner except in the case of SSSIs. The close season will continue to be imposed on rivers, streams and drains.

Rod Fishing Licences 1995/96

Licences are available from every Post Office in England & Wales.
These licences come into effect on 1 April 1995 and are valid for up to one year (annual licences expire 31 March 1996).

How Can You Help?

Fisheries legislation is vital to protect fish stocks, but the cost of enforcement is significant and uses up funds which could be used to improve fisheries.
Anglers, angling clubs and fishery owners can all help keep the costs down.

- Always carry your rod licence when fishing so that you can show it to a NRA bailiff if asked.
- Fishery owners and angling clubs can make it a rule that anglers produce a valid rod licence before a day or season permit is issued.
- Clubs can make it a rule that all members must show their NRA licence to a club bailiff if asked.
- If you see others committing offences, netting or fishing during the close season report it on the NRA Hotline, giving as many details as you can. Vehicle registration numbers can be very useful.

Rivercall

An information guide for river users providing up-to-date information on river conditions in the North West.

By dialling the number below, river users can access regularly updated information on river flow levels across the region.
The information is collected from the NRA's river flow gauging stations situated throughout the North West and will be of interest to anglers, canoeists, walkers and other river users.
A regularly updated recorded message gives details of river flow levels based on average summertime flows on selected rivers in the North West.

NRA Emergency Hotline

You can help the National Rivers Authority to prevent pollution and protect the environment.

Telephone the emergency hotline to report all environmental incidents, such as pollution, poaching and flooding, or any signs of damage or danger to our rivers, lakes and coastal waters. Your prompt action will help the NRA to protect water, wildlife, people and property.

Printed and bound in Great Britain by
BPC Hazell Books Ltd
A member of
The British Printing Company Ltd